1

INSIDE
WRITING

The Academic Word List in Context

Arline Burgmeier

Rachel Lange

SERIES DIRECTOR:

Cheryl Boyd Zimmerman

English Language Programs
Ohio Northern University
525 S. Main Street
Ada, OH 45810

OXFORD

UNIVERSITY PRESS

OXFORD
UNIVERSITY PRESS

198 Madison Avenue
New York, NY 10016 USA

Great Clarendon Street, Oxford, OX2 6DP, United Kingdom

Oxford University Press is a department of the University of Oxford.
It furthers the University's objective of excellence in research, scholarship,
and education by publishing worldwide. Oxford is a registered trade
mark of Oxford University Press in the UK and in certain other countries

Director, ELT New York: Laura Pearson
Head of Adult, ELT New York: Stephanie Karras
Executive Art and Design Manager: Maj-Britt Hagsted
Content Production Manager: Julie Armstrong
Design Project Manager: Michael Steinhofer
Image Manager: Trisha Masterson
Production Artist: Julie Sussman Perez
Production Coordinator: Christopher Espejo

ISBN: 978 0 19 460116 0

Printed in China

This book is printed on paper from certified and well-managed sources

ACKNOWLEDGEMENTS

Illustrations by: 5W Infographics, pgs. 17, 73, 115 and 117.

*We would also like to thank the following for permission to reproduce the following
photographs*: **Cover,** Paul Souders/Corbis; Radius Images/Corbis; Stuart
Westmorland/cultura/Corbis; Izzet Keribar / Getty Images; Stockbyte / Getty
Images; Thorsten Kraska / Getty Images; Maxim Blinkov / Shutterstock;
Jennifer Gottschalk/shutterstock. **Interior**, p1 Jennifer Gottschalk/
Shutterstock (Background); p1 VIEW Pictures Ltd/Alamy (Offices); p2 VIEW
Pictures Ltd/Alamy; p3 View Pictures Ltd/Superstock Ltd. (Bridge by day); p3
VIEW Pictures Ltd/Alamy (Bridge at night); p12 James Lemass/Superstock Ltd.;
p15 18percentgrey/Shutterstock; p29 hudiemm/Getty Images; p30 Ken Welsh/
Alamy; p31 Gallo Images - Neil Overy/Getty Images; p41 TAO Images Limited/
Getty Images; p43 Henrik Lehnerer/Alamy; p44 Adrian Page/Alamy; p45 Nigel
Spiers/Alamy; p54 Radharc Images/Alamy; p57 UpperCut Images/Alamy; p71
Michiel de Wit/Shutterstock; p72 Eiko Jones/Solent News/Rex Features; p79
Maskot/Getty Images; p82 D. Parer & E. Parer-Cook /Ardea; p85 Mykhaylo
Palinchak/Shutterstock; p99 Digital Storm/Shutterstock; p101 ITAR-TASS
Photo Agency/Alamy; p110 imagebroker.net/Superstock Ltd.; p113 Willyam
Bradberry/Shutterstock; p114 Richard Allenby-Pratt/Getty Images; p127
Minerva Studio/Fotolia; p128 Flirt/Superstock Ltd.; p139 Alliance/Fotolia.

Acknowledgements

We would like to acknowledge the following individuals for their input during the development of the series:

Salam Affouneh
Higher Colleges of Technology
Abu Dhabi, U.A.E.

Kristin Bouton
Intensive English Institute
Illinois, U.S.A.

Nicole H. Carrasquel
Center for Multilingual Multicultural Studies
Florida, U.S.A.

Elaine Cockerham
Higher College of Technology
Muscat, Oman

Danielle Dilkes
CultureWorks English as a Second Language Inc.
Ontario, Canada

Susan Donaldson
Tacoma Community College
Washington, U.S.A

Penelope Doyle
Higher Colleges of Technology
Dubai, U.A.E.

Edward Roland Gray
Yonsei University
Seoul, South Korea

Melanie Golbert
Higher Colleges of Technology
Abu Dhabi, U.A.E.

Elise Harbin
Alabama Language Institute
Alabama, U.S.A.

Bill Hodges
University of Guelph
Ontario, Canada

David Daniel Howard
National Chiayi University
Chiayi

Leander Hughes
Saitama Daigaku
Saitama, Japan

James Ishler
Higher Colleges of Technology
Fujairah, U.A.E.

John Iveson
Sheridan College
Ontario, Canada

Alan Lanes
Higher Colleges of Technology
Dubai, U.A.E.

Corinne Marshall
Fanshawe College
Ontario, Canada

Christine Matta
College of DuPage
Illinois, U.S.A.

Beth Montag
University at Kearney
Nebraska, U.S.A.

Kevin Mueller
Tokyo International University
Saitama, Japan

Tracy Anne Munteanu
Higher Colleges of Technology
Fujairah, U.A.E.

Eileen O'Brien
Khalifa University of Science, Technology, and Research
Sharjah, U.A.E.

Jangyo Parsons
Kookmin University
Seoul, South Korea

John P. Racine
Dokkyo Daigaku
Soka City, Japan

Scott Rousseau
American University of Sharjah
Sharjah, U.A.E.

Jane Ryther
American River College
California, U.S.A

Kate Tindle
Zayed University
Dubai, U.A.E.

Melody Traylor
Higher Colleges of Technology
Fujairah, U.A.E.

John Vogels
Higher Colleges of Technology
Dubai, U.A.E.

Kelly Wharton
Fanshawe College
Ontario, Canada

Contents

The Inside Track to Academic Success

Student Books

For additional student resources visit: www.oup.com/elt/insidewriting

iTools for all levels

The *Inside Writing* iTools is for use with an LCD projector or interactive whiteboard.

Resources for whole-class presentation

> **Book-on-screen** focuses class on teaching points and facilitates classroom management.
> **Writing worksheets** provide additional practice with the genre and Writing Models.

Resources for assessment and preparation

> Customizable Unit, Mid-term, and Final Tests evaluate student progress.
> Answer Keys and Teaching Notes

Additional instructor resources at: www.oup.com/elt/teacher/insidewriting

Building a Future

In this unit, you will

> analyze descriptions of structures and learn how they are used in travel writing.
> use descriptive writing.
> increase your understanding of the target academic words for this unit.

WRITING SKILLS

> Descriptive Language
> Basic Paragraph Structure
> **GRAMMAR** Parts of Speech

Self-Assessment

Think about how well you know each target word, and check (✓) the appropriate column. I have…

TARGET WORDS	never seen this word before.	heard or seen the word but am not sure what it means.	heard or seen the word and understand what it means.	used the word confidently in *either* speaking or writing.
AWL				
🔑 consist	;			
edit			✓	
🔑 locate			✓	
🔑 odd				✓
paragraph				✓
🔑 participate				✓
🔑 project				✓
🔑 site			✓	

🔑 Oxford 3000™ keywords

Building Knowledge

Read these questions. Discuss your answers in a small group.

1. Name some interesting buildings in your city or town. What makes them interesting? Are they popular with tourists?

2. How do new buildings differ from older buildings?

3. When you travel, what kinds of buildings and structures do you like to look at?

Writing Models

Travel writing found on websites, in magazines, and in guide books often includes descriptions of buildings or other famous structures. Read two descriptions from a travel website.

Galaxy Soho

China's capital city, Beijing, has just gotten more interesting! I've been to Beijing many times, but when I went back last month, I couldn't miss the stunning[1] new retail and office space, Galaxy Soho. The unusual design is by
5 Zaha Hadid, an Iraqi architect, and it has just opened. In a city full of tall, rectangular buildings, Galaxy Soho is special and different. It **consists** of four **odd** towers. Each one is tall and round like a beehive.[2] The towers are 15 stories high, and they're made of concrete,[3] metal, and glass. Galaxy Soho is a beautiful
10 work of art. Walkways connect the towers and curve gently like a flowing river. An open courtyard in the middle of the **site** lets natural light into each of the buildings. Overall, I found Galaxy Soho both welcoming and practical.

I **participated** in a tour of Galaxy Soho with a group
15 of foreign journalists. The first three floors of the buildings are for retail shops. The next floors **consist** of offices for businesses. At the top, we enjoyed a cup of tea in one of the cafés and restaurants with an amazing view across the whole city of Beijing.

20 Beijing's central business district and the central train station are both just ten minutes away. Two subway lines meet at Chaoyangmen Station, which has an exit by Galaxy Soho. The central **location** allows convenient access for the people of Beijing. It has already become a popular place to shop, eat, and work.

Galaxy Soho in Beijing, China, is designed by Zaha Hadid.

---

[1] *stunning:* very attractive or impressive
[2] *beehive:* a round structure that bees build and live in
[3] *concrete:* gray, rocklike material for building

The Sheikh Zayed Bridge

On a recent trip to the Middle East, I was pleased to discover a beautiful modern structure by a well-known Iraqi architect. Like most of Zaha Hadid's **projects**, the Sheikh Zayed Bridge **consists** of gentle curves and arches instead of sharp angles, corners, and squares.

5   The bridge is **located** in Abu Dhabi in the United Arab Emirates. It connects the mainland to the island of Abu Dhabi. It is 842 meters long and four lanes wide. Some people have said it resembles a concrete ribbon. Others have said the shape looks like waves. I think the bridge's curved lines represent the hills of the Rub' al Khali Desert's sand dunes.[1] Indeed, the bridge looks almost white in the 10 strong sunlight of the day. At night, however, softly changing colored lights dance beautifully across the bridge's three arches.

The Sheikh Zayed Bridge by day ...

    This important new **site** has brought together Abu Dhabi's desert beauty and Hadid's unique modern style. If you are ever in Abu Dhabi, don't miss this wonderful sight!

... and by night.

---

[1] *sand dunes:* small hills of sand

Descriptive Language

LEARN

Writers use descriptive language to talk about buildings and other architectural structures. They can talk about a structure's size, age, colors, materials, and appearance. Writers might compare unusual structures to something familiar to the reader, using verbs such as *look like*, *resemble*, or *represent* or the preposition *like*.

When you describe a structure, ask yourself these questions:

1. What is the size of the structure?

2. What shape is the structure?

3. What are its colors?

4. What materials is it made from?

5. What does it look like? What does it remind you of?

APPLY

Read the descriptions of Galaxy Soho and the Sheikh Zayed Bridge again. Then complete the chart with the descriptive words and phrases from the box. Some words and phrases describe both structures.

15 stories high	convenient	modern
842 meters long	curved	odd
almost white	interesting	round
✓ amazing	glass	softly changing colors
concrete	metal	unique

	Size	Shape	Color	Material	Feeling/ Opinion
Galaxy Soho					*amazing*
Sheikh Zayed Bridge					

Analyze

A. Reread the models on pages 2–3. What do the writers compare the structures to?

1. Galaxy Soho:

_____

_____

2. Sheikh Zayed Bridge:

_____

_____

B. What does each description contain? Check (✓) all the correct boxes.

	Galaxy Soho	Sheikh Zayed Bridge
1. Interesting or surprising opening sentence		
2. Information about the writer's trip		
3. Name of the architect		
4. Physical description of the structure		
5. Contents of the structure or site		
6. Location of the structure		
7. Writer's opinion of the structure		
8. Recommendation to the reader		

C. Discuss these questions with a partner.

1. Most of the writers' comparisons are to the natural world. Why do you think the writers chose to compare buildings to things found in nature?

2. What verb tenses do the writers use? Why?

3. The first writer uses three paragraphs. What information is in each paragraph?

Word Form Chart		
Verb	**Noun**	**Adjective**
participate	participation	_____
locate	location	located

A. Work with a partner. Use a word from the Word Form Chart to complete each sentence. Use the words in parentheses to help you.

1. Sixth Street is a great ___*location*___ for the new building.

(place)

2. Many workers _____ in building the Great Wall of China.

(worked together)

3. The Eiffel Tower is _____ in Paris.

(placed)

4. We looked everywhere, but we could not _____ the plans for

(find)
   the new building.

5. Thank you, everyone, for your _____. We make a great team!

(the act of working together)

The word *edit* means "to correct" or "to fix." It usually refers to the work writers do before publishing what they write.

> The author **edited** her project profile before she put it in her portfolio.

We can also *edit* things that we film, record, or photograph. In this case, when people *edit*, they change the order or remove sections of the work before they release it.

> She directed and helped **edit** several films and television shows.

CORPUS

B. Check (✓) the items that a person can *edit*. Add one more thing that you can *edit*.

  ✓ a book   ____ a movie   ____ a meal

  ____ a broken window   ____ a flat tire   ____ a TV program

  ____ a newspaper article   ____ torn pants   _____

The pronunciation of the word *site* is the same as two other words in English—*cite* and *sight*. Their meanings and spelling are completely different, though.

A *site* is "a place where a building is located" or "a place where something happened."

> This is the **site** where my parents were married.

To *cite* something is "to mention it as an example or as support for what you are saying."

> Ali <u>cited</u> the Sheikh Zayed Bridge as an example of Zaha Hadid's work.

Sight refers to "your ability to see" or "something that you see."

> I have poor <u>sight</u> for seeing distances, so I have to wear glasses.

> We looked out at the beautiful <u>sight</u> of dancing colors on the bridge.

CORPUS

C. Complete the sentences with *cite*, *sight*, or *site*.

1. That building looks like an animal. What an odd _____*sight*_____!

2. If you quote an article written by someone else, be sure to _____ the original source.

3. The reflection of the building in the lake was a lovely _____.

4. This _____ is too small for a shopping mall.

5. My uncle wants to build his house on a _____ near a school.

6. I will never forget the _____ of the Eiffel Tower in the sunset.

7. Can you _____ an example of a building that is used for both housing and offices?

As a noun, *project* (pronounced PRO-ject) means "a plan to do something" or "a piece of work."

> The building **project** will begin soon.

> Raf must complete his research **project** by Friday.

As a verb, *project* (pronounced pro-JECT) has two main meanings:

- to plan or forecast something that will happen in the future
  > We **project** that the building will be completed in two years.

- to make a light or image appear on a screen or wall
  > At night, the city **projects** colorful lights onto the bridge.

CORPUS

D. With a partner, match the beginning of each sentence with the correct ending to form a complete sentence. Take turns reading each sentence out loud. Use the correct pronunciation of *project*.

_d_ 1. The new housing project consists of

2. The company projects a cost of

3. The speaker projected a drawing

4. The company projects that

a. 5 million dollars to build the apartments.

b. construction will begin in 2016.

c. on a screen for the audience to see.

d. 300 new apartments.

Vocabulary Activities STEP II: Sentence Level

E. The words *consist of* tell us what things are made from. Match each item to what it *consists of*. Then write sentences with *consists of*.

_b_ 1. Galaxy Soho

2. concrete

3. the Sheikh Zayed Bridge

4. a paragraph

5. water

a. three curved arches

b. five connected buildings

c. hydrogen and oxygen

d. sand, rocks, cement, and water

e. several sentences about one topic

1. *Galaxy Soho consists of five connected buildings.*

2. _____

3. _____

4. _____

5. _____

Usually, the adjective *odd* means "strange."

*The Royal Ontario Museum in Canada has a very **odd** shape.*

In math, *odd* refers to "a number that you cannot divide by 2." The opposite is *even*.

*The numbers 1, 3, 5, 7, and 9 are all **odd** numbers. **Even** numbers are 2, 4, 6, and 8.*

Odd can sometimes mean "not regular" or "occasional."

*I usually eat a healthy diet, but I do enjoy the **odd** cupcake or two.*

Odd can also mean "approximately" or "about."

*I spend 40 **odd** hours a week in the office.*

CORPUS

F. Answer each question with a sentence using the word *odd*.

1. What makes Zaha Hadid's buildings different?

   Hadid's buildings often have odd, rounded shapes.

2. What do the numbers 67, 29, 11, and 13 have in common?

3. How much time do you spend per day studying English?

4. Describe something strange about a place you know.

5. If you add an even number and an odd number, what type of number will the answer be?

G. Complete each sentence to show what each unit of writing *consists of*. Use the words from the box.

chapters	words	paragraphs
sentences	chapters	letters

1. A word *consists of several letters.* .
2. A book _____ .
3. A paragraph _____ .
4. A sentence _____ .
5. A chapter _____ .

Nouns, verbs, adjectives, and adverbs are all parts of speech. Understanding parts of speech means knowing how a word works.

Nouns are the names of people, places, things, and ideas.

(Galaxy Soho) is an amazing (work) of (art.)

Verbs describe actions or states of being.

It (connects) the mainland to the island of Abu Dhabi.

The Sheikh Zayed Bridge (is) 842 meters long.

Adjectives give you more information about nouns.

In a city full of (tall), (rectangular) buildings, Galaxy Soho is (special) and (different.)

Adverbs give you more information about verbs, adjectives, or whole sentences.

The walkways curve (gently) like a flowing river.

The Sheikh Zayed Bridge is a (truly) amazing structure.

A. Read the sentences. Circle the nouns and box the verbs.

1. At (night), (colors) dance across the (bridge.)

2. The Sheikh Zayed Bridge consists of curves and arches.

3. Most buildings are tall, rectangular, and made of concrete.

4. A courtyard in the middle lets light into the buildings.

5. The wind lifts the sand over the sand dunes.

6. Zaha Hadid grew up in Iraq.

B. Read the sentences. Underline the adjectives and double underline the adverbs.

1. Unbelievably noisy trains rush quickly over the old bridge.

2. This project effectively honors Abu Dhabi's natural beauty.

3. The new bridge appears to float gracefully over the water.

4. Galaxy Soho is an amazingly curved building.

5. That tower looks dangerously tall.

WRITING SKILL — Basic Paragraph Structure

LEARN

Paragraphs are usually several sentences long. The first sentence often tells readers what the paragraph is about. This is called a topic sentence. A topic sentence names the subject of the paragraph and may give the writer's opinion or a main idea about that subject. Supporting sentences give examples or details to explain the main idea. Supporting sentences in a descriptive paragraph help readers picture the place in their minds.

Not every paragraph has a topic sentence. Sometimes short paragraphs in the middle of a text do not need a topic sentence. However, the first paragraph of a text almost always has a topic sentence. The topic sentence is usually near the beginning of the paragraph. Sometimes it is the first sentence, but sometimes a catchy introductory sentence comes first. It is also possible to have the topic sentence last, where it sums up all of the information presented.

To write a descriptive paragraph:

- develop a topic sentence that tells what the paragraph is about.

  The Sydney Opera house is one of the most famous buildings in Australia.

  The Petronas Towers in Malaysia are popular with both local residents and tourists.

- support your topic sentence with examples and details.

- add one or two opening sentences to catch the reader's attention.

When you want to write about a new main idea, begin a new paragraph.

APPLY

A. Work with a partner. Read the pairs of sentences from the writing models on pages 2–3. Write *TS* if the sentence is a topic sentence and *SS* if the sentence contains supporting details.

1. ____ In a city full of tall, rectangular buildings, Galaxy Soho is special and different.

   ____ The towers are 15 stories high, and they're made of concrete, metal, and glass.

2. ____ An open courtyard in the middle of the site lets natural light into each of the buildings.

   ____ Galaxy Soho is a beautiful work of art.

3. ____ Two subway lines meet at Chaoyangmen Station, which has an exit by Galaxy Soho.

   ____ The central location allows convenient access for the people of Beijing.

4. _____ On a recent trip to the Middle East, I was pleased to discover a beautiful modern structure built by a well-known Iraqi architect.

_____ The bridge looks almost white in the strong sunlight of the day.

B. **Work with a partner. Discuss these questions.**

1. Check the location of the sentences in activity A that you identified as topic sentences. Where are they found in the paragraph?

2. Reread the writing models on pages 2–3. What is the function of the first sentence in each paragraph?

Collaborative Writing

A. Work with a partner. Look at the picture and read the information about the Seattle Space Needle. Write some sentences using the information on the notecards.

in Seattle, Washington, U.S.A.

184 meters high

steel and concrete

architects Edward E. Carlson and John Graham, Jr., in participation with the 1962 World Fair

visitors go up in elevators

gift shop, restaurant, observation deck at the top

_____

_____

_____

_____

The Space Needle, Seattle, Washington, U.S.A.

B. Work with your class to create a topic sentence for a paragraph about the Space Needle. Your teacher will write it on the board.

C. Work together to write supporting sentences to describe the building. Suggest them to your teacher. Your teacher will write them into a paragraph on the board. Use as many details as possible to help readers picture the building.

Independent Writing

A. Choose a structure you are familiar with that you can describe. It can be a famous building, a bridge, or a local structure that you know. Brainstorm some descriptive language about your structure.

Name of structure: _____

Size	Shape	Colors	Material	Feeling/Opinion

B. Think of comparisons you can make about your structure. Complete the sentences, and then add more ideas of your own.

1. It looks like _____.

2. It resembles _____.

3. _____

4. _____

C. Complete the sentences with information about your structure and site.

1. _____ is located _____.

2. _____ is ___ meters tall.

3. It consists of _____.

4. It is shaped like _____.

5. _____ participated in its construction.

6. At night / During the day, _____ looks _____.

D. Why is the structure interesting? Write a topic sentence to introduce it.

E. Look again at the paragraphs about Galaxy Soho and the Sheikh Zayed Bridge. Circle any descriptive adjectives or adverbs that you could use in your own paragraph.

F. Write the description of the structure that you chose. Start with the topic sentence you wrote in activity D. Then use any appropriate sentences that you completed in activity C. In your writing, use the target vocabulary words from page 1.

VOCABULARY TIP

Use a variety of specific adjectives and adverbs to make your description interesting. For example, instead of *It looks great,* say that it looks *modern, luxurious, futuristic, comfortable, old-fashioned,* or *magnificent.* Use a dictionary or thesaurus to help you.

A. Read your description. Answer the questions below, and make revisions to your description as needed.

1. Check (✓) the information you included in your description.

☐ a topic sentence

☐ supporting sentences

☐ details about the structure's appearance

☐ comparisons to familiar sights in nature or the reader's experience

☐ details about the location and site

2. Look at the information you did not include. Would adding that information make your description more interesting to readers?

Grammar for Editing Capitalizing Proper Nouns

Proper nouns give the names of people, places, and things. When you write a proper noun, use capital letters.

> **G**alaxy **S**oho and the **S**heikh **Z**ayed **B**ridge were both designed by **Z**aha **H**adid.
>
> **G**alaxy **S**oho is in **B**eijing, whereas the **S**heikh **Z**ayed **B**ridge is in **A**bu **D**habi.

You do not need to capitalize general nouns.

> Both structures were designed by the same architectural firm.
>
> The buildings are in different countries.

Notice that all sentences start with a capital letter.

B. Check the language in your description. Revise and edit as needed.

Language Checklist
☐ I used target words in my description.
☐ I used the appropriate part of speech in different parts of my sentences.
☐ I used a variety of specific adjectives and adverbs.
☐ I capitalized proper nouns in the names of places, people, and things.

C. Check your description again. Repeat activities A and B.

Self-Assessment Review: Go back to page 1 and reassess your knowledge of the target vocabulary. How has your understanding of the words changed? What words do you feel most comfortable using now?

Get the Right Advice

In this unit, you will

> analyze advice columns and learn how they are used to help people solve problems.
> use problem-solution writing.
> increase your understanding of the target academic words for this unit.

WRITING SKILLS

> Problem-Solution Organization
> Asking For and Giving Advice
> **GRAMMAR** Compound Sentences

Self-Assessment

Think about how well you know each target word, and check (✓) the appropriate column. I have…

TARGET WORDS	never seen this word before.	heard or seen the word but am not sure what it means.	heard or seen the word and understand what it means.	used the word confidently in *either* speaking or writing.
AWL				
🔑 affect				
🔑 approach				
🔑 challenge				
🔑 concentrate				
🔑 internal				
🔑 medical				
🔑 schedule				
🔑 vary				

🔑 Oxford 3000™ keywords

Building Knowledge

Read these questions. Discuss your answers in a small group.

1. Where do you go for medical advice?

2. Have you ever gotten medical advice from a website? Which websites do you use?

3. Do people write to advice columns in your country? What types of advice do they ask for?

Writing Models

An advice column is often found on a website or in a magazine. Read the following letter from a high school athlete with a problem and the columnist's advice.

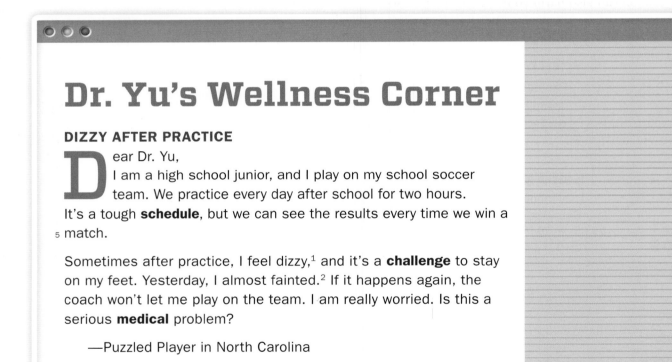

Dr. Yu's Wellness Corner

DIZZY AFTER PRACTICE

Dear Dr. Yu,
I am a high school junior, and I play on my school soccer team. We practice every day after school for two hours. It's a tough **schedule**, but we can see the results every time we win a

5 match.

Sometimes after practice, I feel dizzy,[1] and it's a **challenge** to stay on my feet. Yesterday, I almost fainted.[2] If it happens again, the coach won't let me play on the team. I am really worried. Is this a serious **medical** problem?

—Puzzled Player in North Carolina

---

[1] *dizzy:* feeling as if everything is spinning around you and that you are not able to balance
[2] *faint:* pass out

HYDRATE TO HEAL

Dear Puzzled Player,

I understand that you're worried. I always recommend seeing your doctor when you don't feel well, but your condition is probably not serious. Your body is two-thirds water, and it needs all that **internal** liquid. When you play sports, your body sweats and loses water. This is completely normal. You don't usually notice these small **variations** in the amount of water in your body. However, if you exercise for a long time or in hot weather, you can become dehydrated.[3]

Dehydration is a problem for athletes because it can make you feel sick and even faint. This feeling can **affect** your performance, so you won't run as fast. Dehydration can also harm your **concentration**, so you might not be able to follow the game well! When the amount of water in your body drops a little, fluid[4] moves from your blood into the rest of your body. However, if you don't replace the water, eventually there won't be enough fluid in your blood. Then you could experience very serious health effects.

Fortunately, the solution for dehydration is very simple. When you start to feel the symptoms[5] of dehydration, you just need to drink water. The symptoms **vary** but include dry mouth, headache, and feelings of dizziness. Doctors suggest drinking small amounts of water first. If you try to drink a lot, you could make yourself sick. You can also eat small pieces of ice. If it's hot, you should go inside or sit under a tree where it is cooler.

In the future, you can avoid dehydration by drinking water before you exercise and every hour during your soccer practice. If you feel thirsty, you are already dehydrated, so you need to make sure you are drinking water regularly. You should also **approach** your coach: Other players on your team are probably having the same problem. With lots of water, you can all continue to play your best!

Good luck!

—Dr. Susan Yu ■

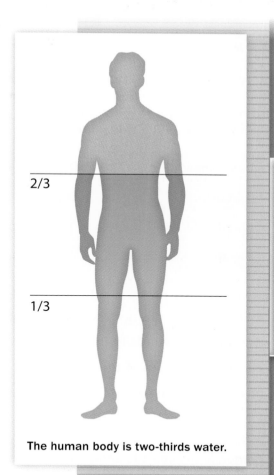

2/3

1/3

The human body is two-thirds water.

---

[3] *dehydrate:* to lose too much water from your body
[4] *fluid:* liquid
[5] *symptom:* a change in your body that shows that you are not healthy

WRITING SKILL Problem-Solution Organization

LEARN

Many types of writing discuss problems and solutions, including advice columns such as the one you read in the writing model. You will also see problem-solution writing in newspaper, magazine, and online articles. Most problem-solution articles follow this pattern:

Background	Describes a situation that leads to the problem
Problem	Describes the problem and tells why it is a problem
Solution(s)	Gives one or more possible solutions
Result	Tells how the solution works

When you write a problem-solution advice column:

- follow the organization: background, problem, solution, result.
- use transition words to introduce each section (e.g., *however* for the problem).
- explain the causes of the problem.
- give at least one piece of advice as a good solution.

APPLY

A. Complete the chart to show how Dr. Yu's response in the the model is organized.

Section	Lines
Background	*2–10*
Problem	
Solutions	
Result	

B. Which words does Dr. Yu use to introduce the problem and solutions in the column?

1. Problem: _____

2. Solutions: _____

Analyze

A. Order the sections of the soccer player's letter from 1 to 5.

_____ Signature

_____ Introduction

_____ Greeting

_____ Problem

_____ Asking for help

B. Answer the questions. Then discuss your responses with a partner.

1. Does the soccer player think his problem is serious? How do you know?

   _____

   _____

2. Does Dr. Yu think the problem is serious? How do you know?

   _____

   _____

3. Why does the soccer player not sign his or her real name?

   _____

   _____

4. Where could you read an advice column like this?

   _____

   _____

C. Should Dr. Yu include any of this extra information in her letter? Circle *Y* for *yes* or *N* for *no*. Discuss your reasons with a small group.

1. Y/N If you faint because of dehydration, you should call a doctor.
2. Y/N If you eat bad food, you can also end up with dehydration.
3. Y/N Sports drinks are better than water if you are dehydrated because they contain salts and vitamins the body needs.
4. Y/N Dehydration is usually more serious for young people than adults.
5. Y/N Although it's rare, it's also possible to drink too much water.

A. Read the sentences about walking. Circle the word or phrase in parentheses that has the same meaning as the underlined word in each sentence.

1. Many doctors suggest that people <u>schedule</u> (learn, (plan,) develop) time every day for walking.

2. Although many people think walking is not very useful, most <u>medical</u> (experienced, educated, health) professionals agree that walking is an excellent form of exercise.

3. Besides helping you lose weight, walking has <u>internal</u> (physical, inner, health) benefits such as lowering blood pressure and strengthening bones.

4. To keep this exercise interesting, <u>vary</u> (keep, check, change) the location of your walks by going to new and different places.

5. While you walk, <u>concentrate</u> (work, focus, keep) on good form. Stand up straight and don't look at the ground while you walk.

B. The verb *affect* means "to make someone or something change." The noun *effect* refers to "the change itself." Complete the following sentences with a form of *affect* or *effect*.

1. Sleep problems can _____*affect*_____ your ability to concentrate.

2. There are many positive _____ of weight loss.

3. Pollution _____ the environment in many ways, and it has negative _____ on human health, too.

4. One _____ of exercise is better sleep quality.

5. Many people do not realize how stress _____ their health.

1. The word *approach* describes "a way of coming near someone or something."

   The best **approach** to Makanaki Hospital is from Sante Street.

   The nurse **approached** the patient with a question.

2. *Approach* also refers to "a way of doing something."

   The hospital uses a new **approach** to pain management.

   The report suggests that doctors **approach** the disease in a new way.

CORPUS

C. Which meaning of *approach* is used in the following sentences?

2 1. The best approach to preventing diabetes is with diet and exercise.

___ 2. If this medicine doesn't work, we will try a new approach.

___ 3. You'll get here faster if you approach the campus from the south.

___ 4. I approached her after the meeting to ask about sleep problems.

D. Use the target vocabulary in the box to complete the advice column. Use the words in parentheses to help you.

approach	challenging	concentrate	medical	schedule

Dear Dr. Yu,

I recently read an advertisement about a new diet. The diet consists of vitamin drinks. The ad says this diet is the only way to get all the vitamins I need. I have a busy ___schedule___, so a simple diet like this would save me
(1. plan of activities)
time. Do you think this kind of diet is a good idea?

—Busy College Student

Dear Busy College Student,

In general, be cautious about taking _____ advice from ads.
(2. health)
However, the ad is correct about vitamins. They are important to your health. According to researchers, vitamins support your immune system, keep your bones strong, and even improve your vision. However, it is best to get your vitamins through a healthy diet.

When you leave for school every morning, put some fruits, nuts, and vegetables in your school bag. These snacks will give you vitamins A, C, E, and K. Breads and cereals can be easy snacks, too. They provide vitamin B. When you sit down for a meal, _____ on eating green
(3. focus your attention)
vegetables. Meat is also an important source of vitamins B and D. And don't forget to drink milk for calcium.

Getting a balanced diet doesn't have to be _____. It can be easy
(4. difficult)
if you snack on healthy foods throughout the day. If you take this

_____ to eating, you will find that you feel both healthy and satisfied.
(5. way)

—Dr. Susan Yu

A *challenge* is "a new or difficult thing that makes you try hard." When something is difficult, you can say it is *challenging*.

> *Studying for the medical exam was a **challenge**.*
> *The exam was **challenging**.*

If you *challenge* someone, you are inviting him or her to a competition, or you are saying that the person is wrong.

> *Alberto **challenged** Mary to a wheelchair race.*
> *Some people **challenge** the idea that meat is necessary for a healthy diet.*

E. Rewrite the following sentences using a form of *challenge*.

1. Antonio invited Raul to race him to school.

   Antonio challenged Raul to race him to school.

2. Diagnosing Miriam's illness was difficult for the doctor.

   _____

3. The scientist questioned the idea that eating chocolate could cure cancer.

   _____

4. It was a problem to read the doctor's instructions.

   _____

1. When you *concentrate*, you "give all your attention to something."

   > *The nurse asked me to **concentrate** on my breathing.*
   > *She'll spend the summer **concentrating** on her new baby's health.*

2. The noun *concentrate* also refers to "the amount of something in a place or substance."

   > *There is a high **concentration** of dentists along the U.S.–Mexico border.*
   > *Fruit juice has a high **concentration** of sugar.*

F. Answer the following sentences using a form of *concentrate*.

1. Why is noise a problem when people study?

   It is difficult to concentrate when there is too much noise.

2. What types of things distract you from your studies?

   _____

3. In which part of town do most people live?

_____

4. What is the focus of your school studies?

_____

Grammar | Compound Sentences

Good writers use a variety of short and long sentences. This makes their writing flow more naturally. To form longer sentences, writers often join two sentences (independent clauses) together. This is called a compound sentence. To form a compound sentence, use a conjunction such as *and, but,* or *so.*

Use the conjunction *but* to contrast ideas.

Independent Clause   Independent Clause

Children fall asleep quite early, but teenagers often stay up late.

Use the conjunction *and* to add information.

Independent Clause   Independent Clause

Exercise can help, and it is great for general health.

Use the conjunction *so* to show a result.

Independent Clause   Independent Clause

He takes long naps in the afternoon, so he stays up late at night.

A. Complete these sentences.

1. You might not feel thirsty, but _you might still be dehydrated_

_____.

2. Many athletes push themselves hard during a game, so _____

_____.

3. The player should talk to the coach, and _____

_____.

4. _____, but it isn't a good idea.

5. _____, so it might be difficult at first.

6. _____, and his game will improve.

B. Choose one independent clause from column A and one from column B. Write sentences joining them with the conjunction in parentheses. Then compare your sentences with a partner.

A	B
I couldn't find my phone	I took a walk
I woke up early	I called my classmate
I forgot my homework	it didn't matter
I fought with my friend	I was late
I had nothing to do	I learned my lesson
I missed the bus	I was sorry later
I wanted to have lunch with someone	I called my parents
It was a beautiful sunny day	I apologized

1. (so)

   I fought with my friend, so I was late.

2. (and)

   _____

3. (but)

   _____

C. Read this letter to Dr. Yu. All the sentences here are simple sentences. Change some of the sentences into compound sentences.

Dear Dr. Yu,

My son is eight years old. He loves sweets. He gets out of school. I am at work. He goes to his grandmother's house. His grandmother loves my son very much. She gives him sweets. My son doesn't get exercise. He just plays video games. He is gaining weight. His grandmother continues to give him sweets. Should he go on a diet?

—Fatima in Abu Dhabi

_____

_____

_____

_____

_____

_____

WRITING SKILL — Asking For and Giving Advice

LEARN

Here is some information about writing letters to advice columns in newspapers, magazines, or websites:

- Start your letter *Dear* and the person's name, followed by a comma. Check the advice column to see how the person wants to be addressed—for example, by first name, by last name, or by a nickname. Remember to use a title (*Mr.*, *Mrs.*, *Ms.*, *Dr.*, etc.) with a person's last name.

- Explain your problem and ask your question. Include all the necessary information. The person writing advice has to be able to fully understand your situation.

- Don't include information or stories that are not relevant or important. Other readers (and the person writing the advice) might get bored or confused.

- You don't need a closing such as *Sincerely* or *Best wishes*.

- Sign your letter with your name. Some people want to keep their privacy and not use their full name in public. You can use just your first name (*Jim*) or a short description (*Confused*; *Too Tired to Practice*).

- It's also common to say where you are writing from. You can include a city or country after your name: *Jim in Toronto*; *Confused in Canada*; *Too Tired to Practice in Kuala Lumpur*.

APPLY

A. Underline the greeting, closing, and signature in both letters in the writing model on pages 16–17 and activity C on page 24.

B. Reread the writing model. Answer the questions with a partner.

1. Did Puzzled Player give too much information about the problem, not enough information, or just the right amount? Would you suggest deleting or adding anything? If so, what?

2. Did Dr. Yu give too much information about the problem, not enough information, or just the right amount? Would you suggest deleting or adding anything? If so, what?

Collaborative Writing

A. Read the letter to Dr. Yu from Nick. Work in a small group. Discuss how you would respond to Nick.

Dear Dr. Yu,

I participate in college track and field. At first, I was getting stronger and faster. That has changed. I stopped making progress, and I'm getting worse! I train at the same time every day. I have a challenging training routine, and I haven't changed it. Still, I'm not improving. I am tired all the time, and I feel like giving up. What should I do?

—Nick in Seoul

B. With a partner, write a response to the letter from Nick in activity A. Use the ideas you discussed. Be sure to clarify the problem, share some possible causes, suggest some approaches to solving the problem, and end with key advice.

C. Share your responses with the class. Then discuss these questions.

1. What causes did the different pairs give?

2. What solutions did each pair give?

3. How did each column's key advice differ from the others?

Independent Writing

A. Choose a health problem for which someone would ask for help by writing to an advice column.

Use one of the following situations or your own idea:

- you keep falling asleep in class

- you are too busy to exercise

- you want to eat healthier food, but you don't know what to choose or how to cook

- you put off doing important assignments until the last minute and then don't have time to do them properly

- you study hard, but you get very nervous during exams and perform poorly

B. Write a letter explaining your problem. Then exchange letters with a partner. Choose a partner who wrote about a different problem, if possible.

C. Use the graphic organizer below to brainstorm ideas for a response to your partner's letter.

Show you understand the problem. • Calm the writer's fears. or • Express the seriousness of the problem.	
Explain the causes of the problem.	
Give possible solutions to the problem.	

D. Look back at the words of advice used in this unit. Circle any language you could use when you give advice.

E. Write your advice column to respond to your partner's problem. Use the graphic organizer to help you organize your information. In your writing, use target vocabulary words from page 15 and include helpful words and phrases of advice from the Vocabulary Tip box.

> **VOCABULARY TIP**
>
> Here are some phrases for giving advice:
>
> *I advise/suggest that you . . .*
>
> *You should/should not [verb]*
>
> *. . . can be helpful/ dangerous.*
>
> *Consider [verb+ing]*
>
> *It is best to (verb).*
>
> *One solution is . . .*

A. Read your advice column. Answer the questions below, and make revisions to your advice column as needed.

1. Check (✓) the information that you included in your advice column.

☐ a restatement or clarification of the problem

☐ sentences to calm the reader's fears

☐ possible causes of the problem

☐ possible solutions

☐ a key point for the reader to remember

☐ a final recommendation about what to do

2. Look at the information you did not include. Would adding that information make your advice column more helpful to readers?

Grammar for Editing Run-On Sentences

When writers join two independent clauses without using correct punctuation, they can create a run-on sentence. There are two ways to edit run-on sentences.

Run-On Sentence

My daughter eats too much candy she is getting cavities in her teeth.

First Solution

Divide the run-on sentence into two separate sentences.

My daughter eats too much candy. She is getting cavities in her teeth.

Second Solution

Join the clauses with a comma and a conjunction.

My daughter eats too much candy, so she is getting cavities in her teeth.

B. Check the language in your advice column. Revise and edit as needed.

Language Checklist
☐ I used target words in my advice column.
☐ I used a variety of phrases to give advice.
☐ I used conjunctions to combine sentences.
☐ I fixed any run-on sentences I found in my writing.

C. Check your advice column again. Repeat activities A and B.

Self-Assessment Review: Go back to page 15 and reassess your knowledge of the target vocabulary. How has your understanding of the words changed? What words do you feel most comfortable using now?

Marketing in Color

In this unit, you will

> analyze summaries and learn how they are used to demonstrate understanding of an article.
> write a summary to retell main ideas.
> increase your understanding of the target academic words in this unit.

WRITING SKILLS

> Main Ideas and Details
> Summarizing
> **GRAMMAR** Gerunds

Self-Assessment

Think about how well you know each target word, and check (✓) the appropriate column. I have…

TARGET WORDS	never seen this word before.	heard or seen the word but am not sure what it means.	heard or seen the word and understand what it means.	used the word confidently in *either* speaking or writing.
AWL				
🔑 aware				
🔑 communicate				
🔑 contact				
🔑 legal				
🔑 method				
🔑 specific				
🔑 summary				
🔑 trend				

🔑 Oxford 3000™ keywords

Building Knowledge

Read these questions. Discuss your answers in a small group.

1. What are the names of some of the supermarkets in your area?

2. What colors do they use in their store signs?

3. Do you think the color of the signs is important? Why or why not?

Writing Model

An article summary gives the most important ideas in an article. Read the article about the power of color. Then read the summary.

Why Red Is Best

by Jennifer Bixby

If you look at the logos[1] of the top supermarkets in the United States, they all have one thing in common: red. These businesses use red in their logos, in product
5 packaging, and in advertising. Marketing experts in the food industry understand that colors affect customers. For that reason, red is the most common color in supermarket brands and logos. But why is red best?

10 Color psychologists report that the color red increases a person's appetite. You may not be **aware** of being hungry, but red does stimulate[2] appetite. Experts say this is because many nutritious[3] fruits and vegetables are red. If
15 supermarket shoppers see red and feel hungry while they shop, they will buy more. So advertisers understand that red is good for business. According to studies, red also quickly attracts a person's attention. In addition, it

The color red can be good for business.

20 makes a person excited and increases the heart rate. Using red helps supermarkets **communicate** that they are energetic, positive places to shop. For these reasons, red is a perfect color for a supermarket brand. It is a
25 subtle[4] but **legal method** for influencing customers.

A recent **trend**, however, has resulted in a new color for supermarket logos and brands.

---

[1]*logo:* symbol or design used to advertise a company
[2]*stimulate:* to make something more active
[3]*nutritious:* very good for you
[4]*subtle:* not very noticeable

With the increasing demand for organic[5] foods,
30 new natural foods supermarkets have become
popular. They sell natural ingredients and healthy
food products. These supermarkets are using
green in their logos, not red. This is because the
color green reminds people of nature, a clean
35 environment, and healthy foods. Natural food
supermarkets make sure that customers are
aware of how healthy their products are. By
choosing green for the logo, the company creates
a **specific** image and identity.
40   *For additional information about color
psychology,* **contact** *the author at
jbixby@oup.org.*

---

[5]*organic:* food produced using natural methods, not chemicals

Green symbolizes nature.

Summary

    In her recent article "Why Red Is Best," Jennifer Bixby discusses the use of red in
supermarket marketing. Red is the most common color for supermarket logos for several
reasons. First, the color red increases your appetite, according to experts. Shopping while
you are hungry will result in buying more food. Second, red attracts your attention and
5 makes you excited. Supermarkets use red because it **communicates** energy and
excitement to the customer. The author also writes about new supermarkets that sell
natural foods. These kinds of supermarkets often use green in their logos. Green suggests
nature, the environment, and health, and that is the message that those supermarkets want
to send to customers.

LEARN

A summary is a short description of the main ideas of an article. A good summary gives only the most important information. When you summarize an article, first identify the main ideas and the important supporting details or examples to include in your summary. Don't include minor (less important) details.

To select the most important ideas to include in your summary, follow these steps:

- Read the whole article and be sure you understand it. Check any unfamiliar words in a dictionary if necessary.

- Ask yourself, "What is the main message of this article? What is the most important point the writer is trying to make?"

- In each paragraph, underline the topic and the main idea of that paragraph. The main idea might be stated in more than one sentence.

- Details will usually be specific examples or further explanations of the broader main idea. Examples and explanations help you understand the main idea, but the main idea itself can be expressed without them.

APPLY

A. Reread the summary on page 31. Begin with the second sentence. Label each sentence in the summary with the paragraph number from the article that each sentence relates to.

B. Check (✓) which ideas are included in the original article and which are included in the summary.

	Original article	Summary
The name of the author and the title of the original article	✓	✓
Supermarkets use red in product packaging.		
Color psychologists say that red increases a person's appetite.		
If shoppers feel hungry, they will buy more food.		
The color red quickly attracts your attention.		
Using red in advertising is legal.		
Organic food is becoming more popular now.		
New natural foods supermarkets use green in their logos.		
Green suggests nature and health.		
Companies create a specific image by choosing the color green.		

Analyze

A. Complete the outline of the summary on page 31.

Article title: _____

Author: _____

    A. Topic: _____

    B. Reasons red is the most common color used in supermarkets

        1. _____

        2. _____

    C. New supermarkets

        1. They sell _____ food.

        2. They use _____ logos.

            a. nature

            b. _____

            c. _____

B. Answer the questions. Discuss your answers with a partner.

1. In the second paragraph, who are the experts in this sentence? *Experts say this is because many nutritious fruits and vegetables are red.*

2. Do you believe the statements made in the article? For example, do you believe that red increases the appetite and attracts attention? Why or why not?

3. The article does not have facts or statistics about the studies or science of color psychology. Do you think the article would be stronger with that information? Would you include the facts in a summary? Why or why not?

C. What is the purpose of this summary? Check (✓) the statements that are correct.

____ 1. It explains the article for someone who hasn't read it.

____ 2. It gives the summary writer's opinion.

____ 3. It shows that the summary writer understood the article.

____ 4. It combines information from the article with information from other sources.

____ 5. It proves or disproves the information in the original article.

1. As a verb, *contact* means "to call or write to someone."

   *For the survey, the company **contacted** 3,800 marketers in seven countries.*

2. As a noun, *contact* means "the act of communicating with someone." Common collocations are *have contact with, stay/be in contact with,* and *lose contact with.*

   *After he left his position, the manager <u>had</u> little **<u>contact</u> with** his former colleagues.*

   *I <u>stay in **contact** with</u> old friends through email.*

2. *Contact* can also mean "the state of touching someone or something."

   *Babies need a lot of <u>physical **contact**</u> like hugging and holding.*

   *Do not allow this product <u>to come into **contact** with</u> your skin.*

3. A *contact* is "a person you know who may be able to help you, especially in business."

   *The student used the Internet and social media websites to build business **contacts**.*

   *Fatima has **contacts** all over the Middle East.*

 CORPUS

A. With a partner, complete each sentence with a phrase from the box. Discuss which meaning of *contact* is used in each sentence.

business contacts	came into contact with	have any contacts
lost contact	stay in contact with	to contact

1. Would you like us _____<u>to contact</u>_____ you about our promotions?

2. Lynne and I _____ after high school. I haven't spoken to her since graduation.

3. During my hike I _____ poison ivy, and later I developed a terrible rash.

4. We need a web developer. Do you _____ in that field?

5. Cell phones allow family members to easily _____ each other.

6. Some people use social websites to build _____.

B. The words in the box are different forms of the target words. Complete the chart with the word forms used in the writing model. Use a dictionary to check your answers.

Noun	Verb	Adjective	Adverb
awareness	_____	*aware*	_____
communication		communicative	_____
_____	_____		legally
	_____	methodical	methodically
specifics	_____		specifically
	summarize	_____	_____

C. Use the words from the box in activity B to complete the sentences. Use the words in parentheses to help you.

1. I will _____*summarize*_____ the article so you won't have to read all
   (give a short version of)
   four pages.

2. It is not _____ to lie about your product in advertisements. There
   (lawful)
   are laws against false advertising.

3. The survey about Internet use _____ asked about time spent
   (especially)
   playing video games.

4. Jae is very _____ in his research. He does each step in order.
   (careful)

5. I am not _____ of any new trends in marketing. Do you know how
   (informed)
   I could find out more about the latest trends?

6. My cousin is extremely quiet and is not very _____.
   (willing to give information)

D. If something is allowed by law, it is *legal*. If it is not allowed, it is *illegal*. Complete each sentence below with *legal* or *illegal*. Answers may vary.

1. Driving over the speed limit is _____*illegal*_____.

2. Talking on a cell phone while driving is _____.

3. Driving without a seat belt is _____.

4. In my area, it is _____ to smoke in a restaurant.

5. Twenty years ago, smoking on an airplane was _____.

6. You may get a traffic ticket if you do something _____while you are driving.

7. It is _____ to make a copy of a commercial video and sell it to someone.

Vocabulary Activities STEP II: Sentence Level

If you are *aware* of something, you know about it.

> Many people are not **aware** of all the ads they see every day.

The noun *awareness* means "a knowledge of something." It sometimes follows a form of the verb *have*.

> She had no **awareness** of the effects of color in advertising.

> **Awareness** of the importance of organic food is increasing.

CORPUS

E. Rewrite the sentences using a form of *aware*.

1. Many people do not know the difficulties of starting a new business.

   Many people are not aware of the difficulties of starting a new business.

2. Business owners must pay attention to the needs of their customers.

   _____

3. Business owners know about both traditional and new ways of advertising.

   _____

4. Marketing a new product becomes easier when people know about it and its reputation.

   _____

5. New business owners need to know about the costs of advertising when they make a budget.

   _____

A *trend* is "a general change or development."

> A current **trend** is toward smaller cars.

> Ana likes to follow the latest fashion **trends**.

The adjective *trendy* is an informal term for "fashionable or newly popular."

> This new restaurant is very **trendy**. It's always crowded, and there is a long wait for a table.

CORPUS

F. What *trends* are you aware of? Answer the questions, using *trend* or *trendy* in your answer.

1. What is a recent trend in TV programs?

   _____

2. Some fashion trends seem silly. What is a trend from the past that seems funny to you?

   _____

3. What is a trendy fashion this year?

   _____

4. What is the latest trend in cell phones?

   _____

5. What is a new trend in marketing?

   _____

A *method* is "a particular way of doing something." It is commonly followed by *of* plus a noun (*method of studying*).

> My teacher has a good **method** of teaching pronunciation.

The following adjectives often appear with *method: best, new, preferred, scientific, traditional.*

> The **preferred** **method** of payment is by check.

CORPUS

G. Answer each question in a complete sentence. Use the word *method* in your answer.

1. What is your preferred method of communication?

   Email is my preferred method of communication.

2. What is your favorite method of daily transportation?

   _____

3. In what subject area do you use the scientific method?

   _____

4. What is a traditional method of advertising?

   _____

5. What is a more modern method of advertising?

   _____

A gerund is a noun. To make a gerund, use the base form of a verb and add *-ing*. A gerund can be the subject or the object in a sentence.

> Subject: *Marketing* to specific customers can save a company money.
>
> Object: The manager suggested *using* more colorful decorations.

Because gerunds end with *-ing*, they can look like part of a verb phrase. To check whether a word is a gerund or a verb, try substituting another noun its place.

> I enjoy *shopping*. = gerund   ✓ I enjoy music.
>
> I am *shopping*. = verb   ✗ I am music.

Gerunds are often used with prepositions.

> She is thrilled *about learning* a new skill.
>
> I'm sorry *for being* late.
>
> We look forward *to doing* the work.

A. Underline the *–ing* forms in the sentences below. Label them **G** for *gerund* or **V** for *verb*.

      G   G

1. <u>Advertising</u> is <u>marketing</u> that communicates with customers about products.

2. Many companies are advertising on the Internet these days.

3. Internet advertising has its advantages and disadvantages.

4. The biggest advantage is for global companies. Buying ads on a website is often very economical.

5. One disadvantage is that the Internet is overcrowded with ads. Customers are beginning to ignore ads unless they are looking for something specific.

B. Complete each sentence with the correct preposition in brackets ([...]) and the gerund form of the word in parentheses.

1. Randy complained [to, about, for] (do) _____ *about doing* _____ research.

2. Dara is concerned [from, for, about] (do) _____ something wrong.

3. The website won awards [for, on, around] (have) _____ the best design.

4. Our company is used [by, for, to] (be) _____ the best when it comes to marketing.

5. There are many options [on, for, to] (contact) _____ the members of our sales team.

WRITING SKILL Summarizing

LEARN

When you write a summary, or summarize, you use your own words to retell the main ideas and most important information from an article. Someone who has never read the article should be able to understand the essential information just by reading your summary. Your summary also shows that you have understood the main ideas of the article. Because a summary doesn't include minor details, your summary will be shorter than the original article. The summary of a paragraph might be just one or two sentences. The summary of a longer article might be one or two paragraphs.

Follow these steps to write a good summary:

- Make sure you understand the original article.

- Make notes of the main idea and key points without looking at the original article.

- Begin your summary by giving the name of the article and the author.

- Use your own notes to help you explain the ideas from the original article.

- Check your summary against the original. Make sure you have included information correctly.

- Check that you have not used exactly the same sentences as the original.

APPLY

A. Read the paragraph below. Then reread it and highlight the most important information.

A recent study shows that children can recognize company logos before they even begin to read. Children from ages three to five participated in the study. Researchers used the following method for the study. First, researchers showed children logos. Then they asked the children to name the products. Most of the children recognized logos from fast-food restaurants such as McDonald's. They were also aware of logos from entertainment companies. For example, they recognized the Disney logo. Researchers were surprised to learn that children recognized logos for adult products, too. Specifically, they recognized Toyota cars and Shell gasoline.

B. Compare these summaries of the paragraph you just read. Work with a partner. Discuss how the summaries are similar and how they are different. Choose the summary you think is best.

1. Children from ages three to five participated in the study about company logos. In the study, children recognized logos from McDonald's, Disney, Toyota, and Shell. The researchers were surprised.

2. According to a recent study, young children can recognize logos before they learn to read. In the study, children recognized logos from fast-food restaurants, entertainment companies, and even car companies.

3. A recent study shows that children can recognize company logos before they even begin to read. Most of the children recognized logos from fast-food restaurants such as McDonald's. They were also aware of logos from entertainment companies. Surprisingly, they also recognized logos from Toyota and Shell.

C. Look at the two summaries in activity B that you did not choose. How could each summary be improved?

_____

_____

Collaborative Writing

A. Read the paragraph below. Work with a partner to underline the main idea and key points.

Are you interested in starting a business or selling a product? It's important to do some market research first. Research can help you avoid developing a product without a clear market or specific customers. You don't want to spend all your time making something if no one is going to buy it, right? There are many ways to gather information. One way is to conduct a survey about your product. In your survey, you can include questions about pricing, how customers make decisions, and what services or products customers want. Many new business owners think that talking with friends is a good way to get information. Information from possible customers, however, is much more valuable. Before you make the decision to start a business, carefully examine research results. With careful market research, you can offer a product that meets the needs of your customers.

B. Cover the paragraph above. Without looking at the paragraph, tell your partner the main idea in your own words.

C. Work with your partner to summarize the paragraph. Write several sentences, expressing the ideas in your own words.

_____

_____

_____

_____

D. Compare your written summary with another pair of students. How are your summaries similar or different? How can you improve your summary? Make changes to revise your writing.

Independent Writing

A. Read the article below. Then read it again and underline the main ideas.

Fast-Food Marketing Is Unhealthy for Kids

Sebastian Mitchell, *Cornwell Times*

Fast-food restaurants may be cheap, convenient, and, well, fast—but are they a good place to take your kids? Possibly not. And yet, they're trying hard to attract young customers. A recent study by the Yale University Rudd Center shows that fast-food companies are not promoting healthy eating in young children. The study examined food advertising on the most popular children's websites. In one year, they found over 3.4 billion food advertisements on children's websites. They gathered information about the companies and foods in the advertisements. On children's websites, 84 percent of the ads are for unhealthy food. Fast foods contain high levels of sugar and salt. Marketing unhealthy foods to children influences their choices. Even though fast-food companies have agreed to market healthy food to children, this is not happening.

Although many fast-food restaurants have special kids' meals, most of them are unhealthy. For example, in a study of the 12 most popular fast-food restaurants, only 12 out of 3,000 kids' meals were healthy. Most restaurants include french fries and soda with a kids' meal. Experts say that restaurants need to make healthy kids' meals the easiest choice. Clearly, restaurants are marketing unhealthy foods to children, both online and in their establishments.

B. Complete the outline with main ideas from the article to help you write your summary.

Article title: _____

Author: _____

A. _____

B. _____

C. _____

C. Use a thesaurus to look for synonyms for five important words in the article you are summarizing.

D. Write your article summary. Remember to include only the most important information from the article. Use your own words to express the ideas.

> **VOCABULARY TIP**
> Thesauruses list synonyms for different words. Synonyms are words with very similar meanings. For example, synonyms for *communicate* are *talk* and *share*. If you find a word you don't know well in a thesaurus, check a dictionary to see how to use the word in a sentence.

A. Read your article summary. Answer the questions below, and make revisions to your summary as needed.

1. Check (✓) the information you included in your summary.

    ☐ the author and the title of the article

    ☐ the main ideas found in the article

    ☐ key points from the article

2. Did you include any ideas that are too specific? Remove any ideas that are not necessary for understanding the article.

Grammar for Editing | Editing Sentence Fragments

Every sentence must have a subject and a verb. Many also have objects.

> subject   verb
> **Companies**   **advertise.**

> subject   verb   object
> **Companies**   **advertise**   **their products.**

A fragment is a sentence without a subject or a verb.

Add a subject if the sentence is missing one:

> ✗ In the study found that children recognize many logos.

> ✓ In the study, _researchers_ found that children recognize many logos.

Add a verb if the sentence is missing one:

> ✗ Online advertisements a popular way to advertise.

> ✓ Online advertisements _are_ a popular way to advertise.

B. Check the language in your summary. Revise and edit as needed.

Language Checklist
☐ I used target words in my summary.
☐ I used synonyms to express the article's ideas in my own words.
☐ I used gerunds correctly.
☐ I used a subject and verb in each of my sentences.

C. Check your summary again. Repeat activities A and B.

Self-Assessment Review: Go back to page 29 and reassess your knowledge of the target vocabulary. How has your understanding of the words changed? What words do you feel most comfortable using now?

Being Prepared

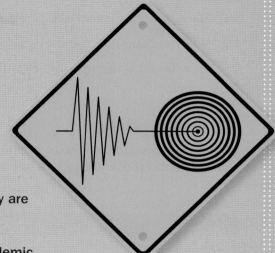

In this unit, you will

> analyze letters to the editor and learn how they are used to express opinions about social issues.
> use support in argumentative writing.
> increase your understanding of the target academic words for this unit.

WRITING SKILLS

> Supporting Opinions
> Topic Sentences
> **GRAMMAR** Modals of Future Possibility

Self-Assessment

Think about how well you know each target word, and check (✓) the appropriate column. I have...

TARGET WORDS	never seen this word before.	heard or seen the word but am not sure what it means.	heard or seen the word and understand what it means.	used the word confidently in *either* speaking or writing.
AWL				
🔑 community				
🔑 contribute				
🔑 generate				
🔑 guarantee				
🔑 maintain				
🔑 primary				
🔑 respond				
🔑 secure				

🔑 Oxford 3000™ keywords

Building Knowledge

Read these questions. Discuss your answers in a small group.

1. Have you ever experienced an earthquake?

2. What are some of the dangers of earthquakes?

3. How could it help people to warn them that an earthquake is coming?

Writing Models

A letter to the editor of a news organization gives an opinion and supports it with reasons. Read these two letters about earthquake warning systems.

LETTERS TO THE EDITOR
EARTHQUAKES: WHEN TO WARN

WHY WAIT UNTIL THE BIG ONE HITS?

Last week's earthquake was yet another reminder that our government must move quickly to approve money for an earthquake warning
5 system. It's obvious that a stronger earthquake could **contribute** to the injury or death of many people in our **community**. Simply put, a warning system would save many lives if people knew that an
10 earthquake was coming.

Earthquake warning systems are already in place in five countries, including Japan. In March of 2011, early warnings of an earthquake gave Japanese residents precious seconds to **respond**, and authorities **maintain** that they saved lives.

15 How would the system work here? Earthquakes **generate** mild underground movements before the severe shaking begins. Motion sensors[1] detect[2] these small movements, enabling special computers to send out warnings. Officials could easily and quickly send warnings by telephone, cell phone, television, radio, and the Internet. People would have 30 to 60 seconds to **respond** to
20 these warnings.

---

[1] *motion sensors:* equipment that detects small movements
[2] *detect:* to notice something that is difficult to feel

Believe it or not, this is enough time to seek safety. For example, train drivers and bus drivers would have time to stop their vehicles. Many lives could be saved.

After all, isn't it the **primary** purpose of our government to **guarantee** the
25 safety of its people? Why is the U.S. so slow to use new technology that is already used in other countries? Why wait until the "Big One" hits?

—*Janice Greenhill, Modesto*

TOO MUCH MONEY, TOO LITTLE WARNING

Although an earthquake warning system sounds like a wonderful idea, it is not a practical[3]
30 solution. There are several reasons why such a system will not work.

The **primary** reason is that 30 to 60 seconds is not enough time to **respond** to a warning. Can you imagine 800 people trying to leave a tall office building in less
35 than a minute? Or hundreds of cars coming to a stop on a crowded freeway? It would be chaos![4] Many people would be injured while others tried to save themselves. In fact, people might be safer if they stayed in the building.

40 Second, there is no **guarantee** that everyone in a **community** would receive the warning. For example, if it came in the middle of the night, most people would be asleep. How could the system notify everyone?

Third, a warning system might **contribute** to a false
45 feeling of **security**. Some people might foolishly believe that the system would give them adequate time to prepare for an earthquake. Can you really prepare in 30 seconds?

Finally, an earthquake warning system would cost many
50 millions of dollars. The government couldn't possibly **generate** enough money to pay for it.

For all these reasons, an earthquake warning system is not a good idea.

—*Ralph Montoya, Stockton*

[3] *practical:* sensible or suitable; likely to be successful
[4] *chaos:* a state of great confusion and lack of order

WRITING SKILL   Supporting Opinions

LEARN

When writing an argument, such as a letter to an editor, writers use a number of techniques to persuade readers to agree with their opinions.

Below are some common techniques that you can use to support your opinion:

1. Clearly state your opinion at the beginning.

2. Focus on a few reasons to support your opinion. Support your reasons with details and examples.

3. Think about the order of your reasons. You can start with the strongest point first or end with the strongest point. Either technique can have a strong impact.

4. Use strong positive or negative words and ideas to get an emotional response from readers.

5. Ask questions that will make your readers think.

6. End with a concluding sentence that restates your opinion or points. As an alternative, you can end with a question.

APPLY

A. Read the letters again. Discuss these questions in a small group.

1. What is the opinion of each writer? Where is each opinion most clearly stated?

2. What reasons does each writer give to support his or her opinion?

3. What examples does each writer use to support the reasons?

4. Compare the two conclusions. Which writer uses a question, and which writer restates the main idea? Which conclusion is more effective? Why?

B. Read these words and phrases from the writing models. Check (✓) the column for the emotional response they create in readers. Which letter has a more negative feeling? Which letter is more effective?

	Positive	Negative		Positive	Negative
injury or death		✓	not a practical solution		
save many lives			not enough time		
easily and quickly			chaos		
guarantee the safety			foolishly believe		

C. What questions does each writer ask?

_____

_____

_____

Analyze

A. Fill in the chart with information from each letter.

Letter 1	Letter 2
Opinion: Last week's earthquake was yet another reminder that our government should build an earthquake warning system.	Opinion: An earthquake warning system sounds like a wonderful idea, but it is not a practical solution.
Reason: It will save lives. Support:	Reason: 30–60 seconds is not enough time. Support:
Reason: Support:	Reason: Support:
Reason: Government should guarantee safety. Support: (none)	Reason: Support:
	Reason: Support: Government cannot generate enough money to pay for it.

B. Discuss these questions in a small group.

1. What is the first writer's strongest reason for building a warning system?

2. What is the second writer's strongest reason for not building a warning system?

3. Where did each writer present his or her strongest reasons? At the beginning or the end?

Vocabulary Activities   STEP I: Word Level

A *community* is "a place where people live" or "the people who live in a place."

> *Several **communities** were without electricity after the earthquake.*

A *community* can also mean "a group of people who have the same culture, interests, or beliefs."

> *The scientific **community** is studying earthquake warning systems.*

CORPUS

A. With a partner, match the people on the left with the *community* they belong to. Take turns making sentences with the information.

_b_ 1. students, professors

___ 2. bankers, store owners, and managers

___ 3. people from China, Korea, and Japan

___ 4. doctors, nurses, and hospital workers

___ 5. firefighters and police officers

a. the health care community

b. the university community

c. the Asian community

d. the public safety community

e. the business community

To *respond* means "to answer" or "to react." The noun form is *response*.

> *I read the editorial, and I wrote a **response**. I **responded** quickly.*

The phrases *to respond to* something and *in response to* something require you to name what you are responding to.

> *Many readers **responded** to the editorial.*

> *Many readers wrote letters **in response** to the editorial.*

CORPUS

B. Use the correct forms of *respond, respond to,* or *response* to complete the paragraph.

The people in yesterday's bus accident (1) ___*responded*___ in many different

ways. The bus driver's (2) _____ was immediate. He pressed the

brake pedal, but the bus did not stop. It crashed into a tree. The bus driver

stayed calm. He called the police and the bus company. The passengers

(3) _____ the accident with emotion. Some shouted. Some cried.

Some shook. A police car (4) _____ the driver's call in minutes.

The police officer asked if anyone was hurt. Most of the passengers

(5) _____ no. However, one woman's (6) _____ was,

"Yes. My back hurts." The officer called for an ambulance. The ambulance

arrived and took the woman to the hospital. Soon another bus came to drive

the other passengers away.

To *contribute* means "to give or be a part of something with other people."
Usually people *contribute* money, but they may also *contribute* ideas, time, or
objects. *Contribute* is often followed by *to*.

    Nine out of ten business owners **contribute** *money* <u>to</u> *charities.*

    Their combined efforts **contributed** <u>to</u> *the success of the show.*

To *generate* something means "to make, create, or cause something."

    Earthquakes **generate** *underground movements.*

    The movie **generated** *loud laughter in the theater.*

In some cases, the two words have similar meanings.

    Cars **generate** *pollution.*

    Cars **contribute** *to global warming.*

CORPUS

C. Use the correct forms of the words *community*, *contribute*, and *generate* to
complete the paragraph.

A recent storm (1) ___*generated*___ very strong winds. The winds

knocked down trees and destroyed a school playground. People in the

(2) _____ wanted to help fix the playground. A group of parents

wrote a letter. They asked the (3) _____ newspaper to print the

letter. They hoped that people would (4) _____ money, time,

or materials to help rebuild the playground. The plan worked. The letter

(5) _____ a lot of support. Several parents (6) _____

hours of their time to build a new sandbox. The local plumber fixed

the water fountains. A toy store installed a new swing set. Other people

(7) _____ money. Children sold cookies to their neighbors. The

sales (8) _____ $200 for the school. Soon children were playing

in their new playground. The (9) _____ was proud of what its

members could do together.

Vocabulary Activities STEP II: Sentence Level

The most common meaning of the word *maintain* is "to keep something
working well or to make it continue at the same level."

Security guards help **maintain** order at large public events.

When you *maintain* an opinion, you keep that opinion even after
others disagree.

The security guards were not able to control the crowds at the soccer game
last night. But I **maintain** that security guards should be at all the games.

CORPUS

D. Answer the following questions about earthquake warning systems. Use the
target word in parentheses. Share your answers with a partner.

1. Do you think local citizens should pay taxes for earthquake warning systems?
   Why, or why not? (community)

   Yes, I do. Earthquake warning systems help the whole community, so everyone

   should help pay for them.

2. Do you think that an earthquake warning system can ensure people's safety?
   Why, or why not? (guarantee)

   _____

   _____

3. Do you think a government's main purpose is to guarantee the safety of its
   people? (primary)

   _____

   _____

4. How can governments keep order during a large earthquake? (maintain)

   _____

   _____

Security refers to "a feeling of being safe." If you feel *secure*, you feel safe and not worried.

> As people grow older, they worry about their financial **security**.

> Children feel **secure** in a happy family.

When an object or situation is *secure*, it is "safe from loss or damage."

> Business is good, so my job is **secure**.

To *secure* something means "to get something, often after much effort."

> It took me ten years to **secure** a university degree.

CORPUS

E. Read the paragraph below. Then answer the questions using the word in parentheses. Compare your sentences with a partner.

Today, young people have a difficult time finding work. This is primarily due to weak economies. After students secure a university degree, they expect to be financially secure adults. Their primary goal is to find a secure job. But many companies are not hiring workers. Young people cannot live on their own if they are not securely employed. Many young people must return to the security of their parents' home.

1. What is the main problem that young people have? (primary)

   Their primary problem is that they cannot find work.

2. What do students expect to have after they earn a degree? (security)

   _____

3. When will young people be able to live on their own? (securely)

   _____

4. Why do young people return to their parents' home? (secure)

   _____

Grammar | Modals of Future Possibility

When you write about the future, you can use modals of possibility. Use modals before other verbs to show levels of possibility. Modals of future possibility include *might, could, would,* and *will.*

Might and *could* express less certainty.

> A warning system <u>might</u> contribute to a false feeling of security.

> The government <u>could</u> save lives by warning people of a coming earthquake.

Would and *will* express more certainty.

Will describes something certain in the future.

> An earthquake warning system <u>will</u> not work.

Would describes something that will happen only under certain circumstances.

> An earthquake warning system <u>would</u> cost millions of dollars (if we built one).

A. Put a minus sign (–) before each sentence that expresses less certainty. Put a plus sign (+) before each sentence that expresses more certainty.

__+__ 1. People would have 30 to 60 seconds to respond to the warnings.

____ 2. Many lives could be saved.

____ 3. People will survive.

____ 4. They would push each other to get out.

____ 5. A warning system might contribute to a false feeling of security.

B. Read each situation below. Then work with a partner to write sentences about what you think will happen next. Use modals in the sentences.

1. Sarkis pours oil into a frying pan. He turns on the stove to heat the oil. Just before he puts food into the pan, his phone rings. He runs out of the kitchen to answer the phone.

   The oil might catch on fire.

2. Hui-Nga has a sociology test on Friday at noon. It is Thursday night, and she is just beginning to study for the test. Suddenly, she remembers that today is her mother's birthday.

3. Leticia and Manuel are from Mexico. They speak Spanish and English. Manuel gets a job in Canada, so they move to Canada. Their daughter, Blanca, is born in Canada. Manuel and Leticia want Blanca to learn English, so they speak to her only in English. They move back to Mexico ten years later.

WRITING SKILL — Topic Sentences

LEARN

In a paragraph, the topic sentence introduces a subject and explains what the writer will say about the subject. A strong topic sentence in argumentative writing clearly states the writer's opinion about the subject.

- A topic sentence is usually found near the beginning of a paragraph. It could be the first sentence, or it could come after a few introductory sentences.

- A topic sentence clearly states one opinion.

- A topic sentence does not state one specific fact or detail, but tells the main idea of a paragraph.

APPLY

Which sentence is the best alternative topic sentence for each letter on pages 44–45? Write your reasons for choosing or rejecting each one.

1. Letter 1

   a. An earthquake warning system is one good way to decrease injuries and deaths from a disaster, but I'm sure there are some other good ways, too.

   _____

   b. There is no reason to wait for another earthquake before we make a decision about an earthquake warning system.

   _____

   c. I believe that we need to be better prepared for earthquakes and that the government needs to set up an earthquake warning system.

   _____

2. Letter 2

   a. There are several disadvantages, such as cost and practicality.

   _____

   b. In my opinion, the government is proposing to create an earthquake warning system.

   _____

   c. We would all like a warning about an earthquake, but the proposed system is not the solution we need.

   _____

Collaborative Writing

A. Read the following notes that a citizen prepared for a letter to the editor of a local news organization. What argument does the writer want to make?

Centerville = small but busy city. Too many cars. Lots of college students walking, riding bicycles.

Cars = noise, pollution, traffic jams

Hard to find parking downtown/parking is expensive

If we had a bus system = solve those problems, also more customers to businesses, safer for pedestrians

B. Work with a partner. Using the notes, write a topic sentence that clearly states the opinion of the writer.

_____

_____

C. Using the topic sentence you wrote for activity B, work with your partner to write a letter to the editor in support of a new bus system.

D. Review your paragraph. Where can you add target vocabulary from this unit?

Independent Writing

A. Read each question below. Choose one of the questions to respond to in a letter to the editor of a magazine or news organization. Choose a question you have a strong feeling about.

- Should high schools require every student to do a set number of hours of volunteer service?

- Should colleges require students to take a physical education class?

- Should governments provide free college education for all citizens?

- Should all citizens in a community pay taxes to run a bus or train system, even if they don't use it?

- Should bicyclists use special bicycle lanes, ride on sidewalks, or share lanes with cars?

B. Brainstorm some ideas for your editorial. Write a topic sentence and then complete the chart with reasons.

Opinion/Topic Sentence:
Reason 1: Support:
Reason 2: Support:
Reason 3: Support:

C. Work with a group of students who are writing on the same topic as you. Discuss the issue and compare your opinions and reasons. Do you agree or disagree? Why? Use the disagreements to make the support for your argument stronger.

D. Complete these sentences to help you introduce reasons and supporting examples.

1. The primary reason for _____ is that _____.
   (opinion)   (reason)

2. For example, _____.
                        (example)

3. Furthermore, _____.
                        (reason)

4. For instance, _____.
                        (example)

E. Write your letter to the editor. Use your idea chart from activity B to help organize your writing. In your writing, use the target vocabulary words from page 43. Include signal words and ideas from activity D.

VOCABULARY TIP

Use these signal words and phrases to introduce reasons and examples:

Reasons

The primary reason …
First, …
Furthermore, …
Finally, …

Examples

For example, …
For instance, …

A. Read your letter. Answer the questions below, and make revisions to your letter as needed.

1. Check (✓) the information that you included in your editorial.

☐ a strong topic sentence that includes the topic and opinion

☐ strong positive or negative words to appeal to readers

☐ at least two reasons to support your opinion

☐ questions that get your readers to think about your opinion

☐ examples to support your reasons

☐ a conclusion that emphasizes the opinion

2. Look at the information you did not include. Would adding that information make your letter stronger?

Grammar for Editing | Common Mistakes with Modals

As you edit your editorial, check your modals carefully. Here are some rules to follow:

1. The verb following a modal must be in the base form.

   Students of architecture *might* <u>enjoy</u> art classes more than students of business.

2. The modal and verb are the same for both singular and plural subjects.

   The school *might* <u>close</u> if it snows. / The schools *might* <u>close</u> if it snows.

3. For negative statements, the word *not* follows the modal but goes before the verb.

   Students *might* <u>not</u> study well on campus.

4. In questions, the subject is between the modal and the verb.

   Would taxes <u>rise</u> to pay for college?

B. Check the language in your letter. Revise and edit as needed.

Language Checklist
☐ I used target words in my letter.
☐ I used signal words to introduce reasons and examples.
☐ I used modals to show future possibility.

C. Check your letter again. Repeat activities A and B.

Self-Assessment Review: Go back to page 43 and reassess your knowledge of the target vocabulary. How has your understanding of the words changed? What words do you feel most comfortable using now?

5

Can Dreams Come True?

In this unit, you will

> analyze personal narratives and learn how they are used in psychology.
> use narrative writing.
> increase your understanding of the target academic words for this unit.

WRITING SKILLS

> Analyzing a Narrative
> Using Hooks
> **GRAMMAR** Present Perfect

Self-Assessment

Think about how well you know each target word, and check (✓) the appropriate column. I have...

TARGET WORDS	never seen this word before.	heard or seen the word but am not sure what it means.	heard or seen the word and understand what it means.	used the word confidently in *either* speaking or writing.
AWL				
🔑 comment				
🔑 conduct				
🔑 demonstrate				
🔑 encounter				
🔑 identify				
🔑 obvious				
🔑 process				
🔑 react				

🔑 Oxford 3000™ keywords

Building Knowledge

Read these questions. Discuss your answers in a small group.

1. Do you sometimes remember your dreams? Did you remember dreams more often when you were young?

2. Why might dreams be important?

3. Why do you think psychologists study dreams?

Writing Model

A narrative describes an event that happened and explains why it is important. Psychology students often write narratives to connect what they are learning with their own experiences. Read this narrative about dreams and memory.

Have I Dreamed That Before?

I've had many strange dreams while I slept. Last week, however, my dream came true. Or did it? My strange dream **encounter** happened this way. I was walking through downtown Greenville on a sunny afternoon. Greenville was my hometown when I was a
5 child. My family moved when I was seven years old, and I've lived in Chicago since then. I could remember our house and my elementary school in Greenville, but not much else. So I was excited to visit Greenville recently for a business meeting. I stayed overnight in a hotel outside of town. When I arrived downtown the
10 next afternoon, I parked in a downtown parking lot. Then, with directions and a map in my hand, I walked down Main Street toward my company's local office.

Suddenly, I stopped in my tracks.[1] I was standing outside the post office, and to my surprise, I vividly[2] remembered the building. I
15 **encountered** it the night before—in my dream! Now I felt like I was living my dream: I could **identify** the bank next door and the stores down the road. In my dream, someone (perhaps my mother) was **conducting** me through the town. She showed me State Street and

---

[1] *stopped in my tracks:* to suddenly stop because something has surprised you
[2] *vividly:* with a strong, clear picture in your mind

Center Road. Sure enough, ahead of me, I could see the street
20 sign at the intersection[3] of Main and State! I didn't need to look
at my map: All of a sudden, it was **obvious** to me to turn right. I
felt very strange. How did I know these things? Did I see the
future in my dream? As I hurried to my meeting, I tried to **process**
this confusing experience. The feeling stopped when I entered
25 the office building. I'm sure my coworkers thought I was reacting
very strangely all day, though! And I have thought about it many
times.

Psychologists have studied this experience. They call it *déjà rêve*,
French for "already dreamed," because you see something and
30 you feel you have already dreamed it. My experience
demonstrates the power of human memory, and, in fact, it is very
common. According to psychologist Alan Brown, 86 percent of
people **commented** in a survey that they have had this feeling.
Here is his explanation. When I arrived in Greenville, I saw a few
35 familiar places from my childhood. Although I didn't really
remember the town at the time, I still had little pieces of old
memories. Because I was in Greenville again, those memories
became part of my dream that first night. Then, the next day,
when I saw the buildings on Main Street, I remembered my
40 dream. But, in fact, I did really know those places; I just didn't
remember them. My dream brought my old memories forward in
my mind. So sometimes our lives remind us of our dreams
because our dreams remind us of our past.

---

[3] *intersection:* a place where two roads cross each other

LEARN

A narrative is a story that has a message, makes a point, or explains something. When you write a narrative, follow these steps:

- Describe the setting in detail so the reader can easily imagine the scene.
- Tell the events of the story in the order that they happened.
- Build the reader's interest as you describe the events leading to the climax. The climax is the most important or surprising part of the story.
- Use a variety of interesting descriptive words.
- End with the message or explanation of the story. Tell what the story means to you and what you learned from it.

APPLY

Reread the narrative. Then answer the following questions.

Setting	1. Where and when did the story take place? _____ 2. Who was there? _____
Climax	3. What was the most important or surprising part of the story? _____
Conclusion	4. How did the story end? What did the writer realize? _____
Explanation	5. Why did the writer tell this story? What did you learn from it? _____ _____

Analyze

A. Answer the questions about the writing model.

1. Which paragraph tells the main events of the narrative? Write down four descriptive words from the paragraph that help build interest.

   _____

2. Which paragraph gives background information about the main events? Why is it necessary?

   _____

B. Number the events below to show the sequence in the story.

_____ I suddenly recognized many buildings on the street.

_____ I returned to my hometown for a meeting and stayed the first night in a hotel.

_____ It was a confusing experience.

_____ I moved from Greenville when I was seven years old.

_____ I realized that I had dreamed about Greenville the night before.

_____ I drove downtown and parked my car. I started to walk to the office building.

C. Discuss the following questions with a partner.

1. What are the main verb tenses used in the writing model? Why does the writer use these tenses?

2. Why does the writer use present tense in the third paragraph?

3. Reread the last sentence in the model. What does it mean? Explain it in your own words.

4. Imagine that the writer only gave the explanation in the third paragraph, and the first and second paragraphs were missing. Would the explanation be as interesting or convincing? Why, or why not?

Vocabulary Activities   STEP I: Word Level

To *conduct* (con-DUCT) something means "to organize or do an activity."

> The tour guide **conducted** a walk through the town.
> The teacher **conducted** a search for the missing notebook.

The noun *conduct* (CON-duct) refers to "the way a person behaves."

> The students' **conduct** showed that they were not interested in the assignment.
> One student was sent out of the class because of his rude **conduct**.

To *demonstrate* something means "to show something clearly." The noun form is *demonstration*.

> The study **demonstrated** the importance of dreams.
> The researcher gave a **demonstration** of how to tell when a sleeper is dreaming.

To *demonstrate* also means "to walk or stand in public with a group of people to show that you have strong feelings about something." A *demonstration* is a protest, and *demonstrators* are protesters.

> The students **demonstrated** in front of the school for lower tuition fees.
> Every year, **demonstrators** march through the school halls.
> The students held a **demonstration** for lower tuition fees.

CORPUS

A. Use the correct forms of *conduct* and *demonstrate* to complete the paragraphs. Use the words in parentheses for help.

Scientists often _____*conduct*_____ experiments with animals. For example,
        (1. organize)

in one experiment scientists used animals to _____ how animals
                                          (2. show)

learn. The scientist rang a bell every time she gave an animal some

food. Soon the animal learned to ring the bell when it wanted food. The

experiment provided a clear _____ that animals can learn.
                          (3. evidence)

Sometimes people _____ in front of laboratories that experiment
                 (4. protest)

with animals. They are worried that the _____ of the scientists
                                       (5. behavior)

will harm the animals. When this happens, scientists sometimes invite the

_____ into the laboratory. The scientists _____ how they
(6. protesters)   (7. show)

use the animals. They explain that the experiments they _____ do
                                                       (8. do)

not harm the animals.

B. The words in the box are synonyms for the target words below. Match each synonym to the target word with the same meaning. Use a dictionary or thesaurus for help.

~~behavior~~	reply	mention	protest
do	show	statement	response

conduct	comment	demonstrate	reaction
behavior			

When you *encounter* something, you experience it. *Face* and *meet* are synonyms for *encounter*.

> If you **encounter** a bear in the woods, back away slowly.

When you *identify* someone, you know who the person is. You can *identify* objects, too. A synonym for *identify* is *recognize*.

> I could **identify** my best friend in the old photo, but I could not **identify** the other kids.

When you *react* to something, you say or do something in response to what has happened. *Respond* is a synonym for *react*. *Response* is a synonym for *reaction*.

> The teacher **reacted** to my comment with a smile. Her **reaction** surprised me.

 CORPUS

C. Work with a partner. Use the correct forms of *encounter*, *identify*, and *react* to complete the paragraph.

Newborn babies quickly learn to _____*identify*_____ their mothers. When
(1. recognize)

a baby hears his mother's voice, the baby _____ by kicking or
(2. responds)

waving his arms. However, if the baby _____ a stranger, he might
(3. meets)

cry. A baby can also _____ his mother by smell. Mothers hold their
(4. know)

babies close to their bodies, so a baby knows her special smell. In a few

months, the baby will be able to _____ his mother by sight. When
(5. recognize)

the baby sees her, his _____ will be a big smile.
(6. answer)

Vocabulary Activities STEP II: Sentence Level

D. Work with a partner. Match each item from the first column with what the person *encountered* in the second column. Write sentences with the word *encountered*.

_a_ 1. The teacher was surprised
when he

____ 2. Yumi knocked loudly when she

____ 3. Ana was worried when she

____ 4. The taxi driver turned around
when he

   a. a student cheating on a test.

   b. a traffic accident.

   c. a locked door to the school's office.

   d. delays at the airport.

1. _The teacher was surprised when he encountered a student cheating on a test._

2. _____

3. _____

4. _____

E. A *process* is a number of actions, one after the other, for doing or making something. Make a list of steps students use in the *process* of learning new words.

1. _They read or hear a word._

2. _____

3. _____

4. _____

5. _____

F. When something is *obvious*, it is easy to see or understand. For each situation below, write a statement about what you think is *obvious*. Use the form of the word that is in parentheses.

1. The little girl was coughing and sneezing. She had a high temperature. (obvious)

   It was obvious that she didn't feel well.

2. Bao drank three glasses of orange juice. (obviously)

   _____

3. The book was torn and faded. It had been printed in 1885. (obviously)

   _____

4. Aisha kept yawning. Her eyes were almost closed, and her head kept nodding. (obvious)

   _____

5. The little boy screamed when he saw the horse. He hid behind his mother and cried. (obvious)

   _____

Grammar | Present Perfect

Use the present perfect to link an event in the past to the present time. Sentences that show an action or idea that continues in the present sometimes use *for, since,* or *always.*

1. The present perfect can show that the event started in the past but is continuing in the present.

   Psychologists *have done* interesting research on dreams.

   I *haven't remembered* any dreams *since* I moved last month.

2. Use the present perfect to express an idea that has continued over a period of time. The exact period of time is unknown or not important.

   People *have always wondered* what dreams mean.

3. Use the present perfect to express an action that has (or has not) happened repeatedly in the past. The exact time is not important or is unknown.

   I've visited that building several times.

   I've never been to that place before.

Form the present perfect with *have/has* + a past participle form of a verb. The form of *have* changes with the person.

For most verbs, the past participle form is the same as the simple past tense form.

A. Look back at the writing model on page 58–59. Underline the sentences that use the present perfect.

B. Write one sentence from the writing model that shows each reason for using the present perfect.

1. An idea that has happened repeatedly over an unspecific period of time

   _____

2. An event that started at a specific time in the past and is continuing into the present

   _____

3. An idea or event that has continued over a period of time

   _____

C. Complete this paragraph by using the present perfect of the verbs in parentheses.

I turned on my favorite television program last night. I ___*have watched*___
(1. watch)

this detective program many times. It used to be my favorite show. Now

I _____ to dislike it. There are so many advertisements. They
(2. start)

_____ the story. I _____ several complaints to the
(3. ruined)   (4. submit)

television station. The station manager _____ me every time.
(5. answer)

She _____. She _____ to show fewer advertisements.
(6. apologize)   (7. promise)

But nothing _____. The advertisements continue. I guess I
(8. change)

should stop watching the program. It only makes me angry.

D. Answer these questions. Use the present perfect.

1. How many times have you been late to class this month?

   _____

2. How many units have you completed in this book?

   _____

3. How long have you studied at this school?

   _____

4. How long have you lived in your current home?

   _____

5. How long have you known your best friend?

   _____

6. How long have you lived at your current address?

   _____

WRITING SKILL   Using Hooks

LEARN

A hook is one or two sentences at the beginning of a paragraph that catch the interest of the reader. It "hooks" the reader's interest and motivates the reader to keep reading. Hooks are useful in narrative writing because you are telling a story. You want to engage the reader from the start. Here are some tips for using and writing hooks:

1. Write your narrative first. Be clear about the main point of your narrative. Then go back and brainstorm ideas for a hook.

2. Usually a hook is used at the beginning of the narrative. Of course, do not use hooks for every paragraph.

3. Write several different kinds of hooks and then choose the best one for your paragraph. You can:

   • Use a statement that presents an interesting point of view or detail. It should make readers curious to read more.

   I've read that, in dreams, we can only see the faces of people we already know.

   • Use a question that will interest readers or make them think. However, don't use questions that are very easy to answer or that have no answer.

   ✓ *How often do you remember your dreams?*
   ✓ *Do you know how many dreams the average person has every night?*
   ✗ *What does "dream" mean?*
   ✗ *Do you know what my favorite dream is?*

   • Give an interesting or surprising statistic or general fact about your topic. It should make readers curious to read more.

   Studies have shown that people forget 90 percent of their dreams.

APPLY

Find the hook in the writing model. Reread it and answer the questions.

1. Does the hook use a statement, a question, or an interesting fact?

2. What word in the hook tells you the topic of the narrative?

3. Why is the hook effective? In other words, how does it make you interested to read more?

Collaborative Writing

A. Read the writing assignment and the personal narrative below it. What is the purpose of each paragraph in the narrative? Discuss your answer with a partner.

Childhood memories help us construct our personal life stories and understand ourselves. These memories help us understand who we are and where we come from. Recent studies have shown that for most adults, their earliest memories only date back to early school age. On the other hand, children ages six to nine can remember back to when they were four years old. As children get older, they forget these memories. Write a personal narrative describing an early childhood memory. How old were you at the time? What does the memory tell you about yourself and who you are today?

I was about six years old. It was the first day of first grade, and my mother brought me to school. The classroom was crowded and noisy, with several kids behaving badly. I was surprised. I remember that I just kept my mouth shut and watched what was happening. Because I was so quiet, I was placed in the class for the slower learners. I remember thinking that this was a really boring first grade class. After two weeks, the teacher changed me to a more challenging class.

Although I have tried to remember earlier times in my childhood, this is one of my earliest memories. It is typical for adults to only remember to age five or six. For me, this memory of first grade relates clearly to who I was then and who I am today. I came from a quiet family, and I was very shy. Whenever I wasn't sure what to do or when I lacked confidence, I just didn't say anything. As an adult, I have learned to speak out and I am not shy anymore. I have often thought back to my childhood and have been surprised at my shyness. This memory shows how I have changed over the years.

B. The personal narrative does not have a hook. With a partner, write three different hooks: an interesting statement, a question, and an interesting fact. You may need to revise the first sentences of the narrative to fit in your hook.

_____

_____

_____

_____

_____

_____

_____

_____

C. In a small group, share your hooks. Which hook is the most effective? Why?

Independent Writing

A. Brainstorm a list of three memories or dreams. Choose one to write about. Make a timeline of events.

B. Use this chart to organize your writing. Answer the questions.

Setting	1. Where and when did the story take place?
	2. Who was there?
Climax	3. What was the most important or surprising part of the story?
Conclusion	4. How did the story end? What did you realize?
Explanation	5. Why did you tell this story? What do you want a reader to learn from it?

C. Write your personal narrative. Use the chart in activity B to decide the order of your ideas. In your writing, use the target vocabulary words from page 57. Remember to include descriptive language to make your narrative more interesting.

D. Reread the beginning of your personal narrative. Do you have a hook to engage the reader's interest? Can you improve your hook? Make revisions as needed to finalize your writing.

A. Read your personal narrative. Answer the questions below, and make revisions to your narrative as needed.

1. Check (✓) the information you included in your personal narrative.

   ☐ an interesting hook

   ☐ the setting

   ☐ the events and climax

   ☐ an explanation of how the events relate to psychology

   ☐ what you learned

2. Look at the information you did not include. Would adding that information make your narrative more interesting or helpful to readers?

Grammar for Editing | Common Spelling Errors

In regular verbs, the past (-*ed*) form and the past participle form are the same. Follow these rules for the correct spelling of verbs.

1. If the verb ends in -*e*, add -*d*.

   exercise → exercised   dance → danced

2. If the verb ends in a vowel + consonant, double the consonant and add -*ed*.

   stop → stopped   shop → shopped

3. It the verb ends in two consonants, just add -*ed*.

   end → ended   comment → commented

B. Check the language in your personal narrative. Revise and edit as needed.

Language Checklist
☐ I used target words in my personal narrative.
☐ I used descriptive language.
☐ I used the present perfect correctly.
☐ I spelled verbs correctly.

C. Check your personal narrative again. Repeat activities A and B.

Self-Assessment Review: Go back to page 57 and reassess your knowledge of the target vocabulary. How has your understanding of the words changed? What words do you feel most comfortable using now?

The Wild World of Animals

In this unit, you will

> analyze test responses and learn how they are used in science courses.

> use factual writing.

> increase your understanding of the target academic words for this unit.

WRITING SKILLS

> Analyzing Test Questions and Responses
> Selecting Relevant Information
> **GRAMMAR** Count and Noncount Nouns

Self-Assessment

Think about how well you know each target word, and check (✓) the appropriate column. I have...

TARGET WORDS	never seen this word before.	heard or seen the word but am not sure what it means.	heard or seen the word and understand what it means.	used the word confidently in *either* speaking or writing.
AWL				
🔑 annual				
🔑 decline				
🔑 distribute				
🔑 environment				
🔑 release				
🔑 select				
sequence				
🔑 similar				
🔑 source				
🔑 transfer				

🔑 Oxford 3000™ keywords

Building Knowledge

Read these questions. Discuss your answers in a small group.

1. What words can you think of to describe a frog?

2. Where do frogs live?

3. What do you know about how a frog develops?

Writing Models

A test response demonstrates what a student knows about a subject. Read these responses from a science test about frogs.

Science 214 Our Animal World

Unit: Frogs   Test 4

1. DESCRIBE THE STAGES IN THE DEVELOPMENT OF FROGS. USE THE IMAGES TO HELP YOU.

Tadpoles swim underwater.

Frogs develop in a **sequence** of four stages. First, the female frog
5 **selects** a place to lay her eggs during the **annual** egg-laying season. Usually this is in water or on wet sand. After the female **releases** the eggs, the male fertilizes[1] them,
10 and this is the second stage of the frog's life. If the female lays the eggs on sand, the male frog **transfers** them to a nearby pond or lake. The male then **distributes** the eggs in
15 the water. Soon the eggs hatch into the third stage, tiny tadpoles. A tadpole is **similar** to a fish. It is shaped like a fish, has a tail, and breathes through gills.[2] Like a fish, it lives underwater. In a short time, the tadpole begins
20 to grow arms and legs. It loses its tail. Skin grows over its gills, and lungs develop inside the body. Then the tadpole has to swim to the surface of the water to breathe oxygen into its tiny lungs. Finally, the frog becomes an adult. It is ready to walk and to live on land.

---

[1] *fertilize:* to put a male seed into an egg
[2] *gill:* an airhole on each side of a fish or tadpole that it breathes through

The life cycle of a frog

2. HOW DO FROGS PROTECT THEMSELVES FROM DANGER?

25   Frogs protect themselves in three ways, so they do not become a **source** of food for hungry animals in the **environment**. First, they protect themselves by hiding during the day when predators[3] are looking for them. This also protects them from the hot sun. Second, some frogs fill their bodies with air to look bigger. Third, and most unusually, some frogs **release** a poison through their skin. The poison has a terrible taste. The frog's
30 enemies stop eating the frog because of the bad taste. In these ways, even small frogs can survive in a dangerous **environment**.

3. WHY HAS THERE BEEN A DECLINE IN THE FROG POPULATION[3] IN RECENT YEARS?

    There are three reasons for a **decline** in the frog population. A changing climate is
35 the primary reason. Frogs are widely **distributed** throughout warm areas of the world. Most of these areas have experienced a **decline** in rainfall. Lakes and ponds are drying up. This means there are fewer tadpoles during the **annual** egg-laying season. At the same time, temperatures are rising in these areas. This makes the air hot and dry. Frogs need water in the **environment** to keep their skin wet. Frogs breathe through both their
40 lungs and their skin. When the air is hot and dry, their skin dries out, and they cannot breathe. Another reason for the **decline** is the development of land for industry, farming, housing, airports, and cities. As people develop the land, there is less land available for frogs and other wildlife. This has also generated air pollution, which harms frogs. Finally, eating frog meat has become popular for humans.

---

[3] *predator:* an animal that kills and eats other animals
[4] *frog population:* the number of frogs in the world

LEARN

The first step in answering a test question is to understand the question. Look for keywords. They tell you how to answer the question.

If the question asks you to ...	You will need to ...
describe	give stages or features
explain how	give steps or methods
explain why	give reasons

Follow these steps when you write your answer:

- Use words from the test question to write the first sentence.

  Frogs develop in a sequence of four stages.

- Choose accurate information from your notes or memory.

- Put the information in the correct order (e.g., start with the most important reason, or what happens first).

- Use transition words to organize your answer (*the first reason, the next step*).

- Answer the entire question, but do not include unnecessary information.

APPLY

A. Read the test questions again. Underline the key words. Match the question number with the correct type of answer.

____ Question 1   a. Reasons

____ Question 2   b. Stages

____ Question 3   c. Methods

B. Read the answers again. Circle the transition words that organize each answer. Complete the chart below.

Question 1	Stages in the development of a frog	1. Female lays egg 2. Male fertilizes egg 3. _____ 4. _____
Question 2	Ways frogs protect themselves	1. _____ 2. Fill bodies with air 3. _____
Question 3	Reasons for the decline in the frog population	1. _____ 2. _____ 3. Eating frog meat

Analyze

A. The student thought about adding these sentences to the answer to question 1. Do you think these sentences are useful or not? Discuss your reasons with a small group.

1. Y /(N) There is a lot of rain during the annual egg-laying season.

    This sentence does not answer the question about the stages of a frog's life.

2. Y / N Female frogs lay thousands of eggs.

3. Y / N The pile of eggs is called frogspawn.

4. Y / N Frogs come in many different colors, including green, red, and brown.

5. Y / N Frogs take about 16 weeks to develop from eggs to adult frogs.

B. How is the information organized in each answer?

____ Question 1: a. importance   b. sequence   c. interest

____ Question 2: a. how well-known   b. how common   c. how effective
                          they are   they are   they are

____ Question 3: a. importance   b. time   c. process

C. Discuss these questions with your class.

1. Who will read these answers? How does that affect the way the student wrote the answers?

2. How are these answers different from a description of frogs in a science magazine?

Vocabulary Activities   STEP I: Word Level

A. A *source* is "a person, place, action, or object something comes from or starts from." Work with a partner. List one or more *sources* for each item. Take turns making sentences with the information.

Source of milk	Source of wool	Source of eggs	Source of honey
			bees

Bees are a source of honey.

B. *Similar* is used to compare things that are alike in some way. Complete the chart with words from the box. Write each word below the target word that has a *similar* meaning. Use a dictionary or thesaurus for help.

alike	free	let go	move	refuse	related	shift	weaken	yearly

annual	decline	release	similar	transfer
			alike	

C. Complete the paragraph with words from the box.

annual	annually	environment	similar	similarly

After winter, the (1) _____ nest-building season begins for birds.

They build many kinds of nests. However, all nests are (2) _____

in one way. They provide a safe place for the mother bird to lay eggs.

(3) _____, they provide a warm home for baby birds. Some birds

build nests high in the branches of a tree. They collect grass and small sticks

from their (4) _____. They weave these into bowl-shaped nests.

Birds that live near a lake or river build a different kind of nest. They make a

hole in the sandy shore. They put grass, small stones, and feathers in the hole

to keep the nest dry. Most nests last just one year. Birds must build a new

one (5) _____.

To *release* a person or animal means "to let a person or animal go free."
To *release* something also means "to stop holding something" or "to make
something available to the public."

Verb   *A laboratory recently **released** some poisons into a river.*

Noun   *The **release** of poisons was an accident.*

Verb   *A newspaper **released** the information to the public.*

To *transfer* something means "to move something from one place to another
or from one person to another."

Verb   *The city zoo will **transfer** two popular elephants to another zoo.*

Noun   *Many people are angry about the **transfer** of the elephants.*

The word *decline* means "to get smaller, weaker, or worse." It can also mean
"to say no to an invitation or an opportunity."

Verb   *My grandfather's health has **declined** recently.*

Noun   *My family is worried about Grandpa's **decline** in health.*

Verb   *Because of bad health, Grandpa had to **decline** an invitation to
go fishing.*

D. **Answer each question using the noun form of the underlined word.**

1. A newspaper <u>released</u> a story about a dangerous new disease. How did
people react?

   The release scared many people.

2. Lakes dry up when rainfall <u>declines</u>. What does this affect?

   _____

3. Octopuses <u>release</u> a cloud of black ink when an enemy approaches. How
does this help the octopus?

   _____

4. Mosquitos <u>transfer</u> malaria from one person to another. When does this occur?

   _____

A *sequence* is "a number of things that happen or come one after another."

> Frogs develop in a **sequence** of stages.

> What is the next number in this **sequence**? 2 4 6 8 10

When things are arranged *in sequence*, they are in a certain order. If they are *out of sequence*, they are not in the correct order.

> I put my vacation photos <u>in **sequence**</u> before I shared them with friends.

> The paintings are displayed <u>in</u> historical **<u>sequence</u>**.

CORPUS

E. Are these lists in the right order? Write *in sequence* or *out of sequence*.

1. January, February, April, March

   out of sequence

2. egg, tadpole, baby frog, adult

   _____

3. 75, 73, 76, 74

   _____

4. D, G, F, E, C

   _____

5. cook dinner, eat dinner, wash dishes, put away dishes

   _____

F. To *distribute* things means "to give them to several people or to put them in several places." The noun form is *distribution*. Rewrite each numbered sentence so that it contains the word in parentheses.

(1) Zookeepers spend many hours every day taking food to animals. (2) The process starts early in the morning. (3) First, the zookeepers deliver raw meat to the lions and tigers. Next, they take seeds to the birdcages. (4) They spread the seeds over a wide area. The birds fight if the seeds are put in one spot. When the zookeepers are finally finished, many of the animals are hungry again. (5) It is time to give them more food.

1. (distributing) *Zookeepers spend many hours every day **distributing** food to animals.*

2. (distribution) _____

3. (distribute) _____

4. (distribute) _____

5. (distribute) _____

To *select* something means "to take the person or thing that you like best." A *selection* is "a person or thing that is chosen." The noun *selection* also refers to "a collection of items from which you can choose."

> The female frog **selects** a place to lay her eggs.

> The frog's **selection** is always near water.

> Frogs have a large **selection** of bugs to eat.

The adjective *selective* means "being careful when choosing."

> A female frog is **selective** about choosing a mate.

CORPUS

G. The following paragraph is about an annual fair. Farmers buy, trade, and sell horses at the event. Rewrite each numbered sentence so that it contains the form of *select* in parentheses.

In the morning, farmers transferred their horses from their trucks to a large barn. (1) There was a large group of horses to choose from. Farmers walked through the barns to see the horses. (2) They wanted to choose a horse to buy. (3) They were very careful about choosing. (4) Soon, Farmer Smith made his choice. (5) He chose a gentle horse that his children could ride.

1. (selection) _____

2. (select) _____

3. (selective) _____

4. (selection) _____

5. (selected) _____

Count Nouns

A count noun names something that you can count. The singular form shows that there is one thing. The plural form shows that there is more than one.

Singular

The **frog** sat by the pond.
An **elephant** approached the river.

Plural

The **frogs** laid eggs in the pond.
Two **elephants** followed.

Noncount Nouns

A noncount noun names something that you cannot count. Noncount nouns do not have plural forms. Noncount nouns are often substances or abstract nouns.

Substances

We breathed in the fresh **air**.
The **water** in the pond looks dirty.

Abstract Nouns

I find **happiness** when I work with animals.
Everyone admires her **beauty**.

Some nouns have both a count and a noncount form.

There are 50 **chickens** on the farm.

The fried **chicken** is delicious.

The count noun *chickens* refers to birds. The noncount noun *chicken* refers to meat.

A. Identify the following words as *C* (count) or *N* (noncount).

____ ant   ____ intelligence   ____ pollution

____ frog   ____ milk   ____ tadpole

____ energy   ____ oxygen   ____ tail

B. Work with a partner. Reread the response to the third question on page 73. Circle five count nouns. Underline five noncount nouns. For each noun, explain how you knew it was count or noncount. Share your answers in a small group.

WRITING SKILL — Selecting Relevant Information

LEARN

An important step in answering a test question is to decide which facts to include in your response. Analyzing Test Questions and Responses on page 74 offers steps that writers should take before responding to a test question. An important part of this process is deciding which facts to include in your response.

- Omit facts that are not related to the question or that do not add important information.

- Divide the remaining facts into categories according to topic.

- Decide if the facts in each group are related to each other. Do any of them repeat the same information? Can two or more facts be combined?

- Decide on the best order for presenting these groups of facts. Present them by order of importance, sequence, or location within a system.

APPLY

A. Read the following notes. They were written by a student in a biology class. She wrote them as she listened to the professor's lecture.

> FROGS
>
> Cold-blooded (can't generate body heat). Have backbone, 4 legs. Heart has 3 parts.
> Breathe through lungs and skin. Have moist skin. Ears hear vibrations in ground.
> Some release poison from skin (scares off other animals). Have big eyes.
> Bright color warns enemies—poisonous.
> Release waste gas through skin.
>
> Warm weather starts egg-laying season every year. Also lots of rain.
> Female lays eggs. Male fertilizes.
> If eggs are laid on dry land, male moves them to water.
> Sequence: eggs → tadpoles → lose gills → grow lungs and legs → lose tail → leave water.
> Live on land in moist areas: need to keep skin moist to breathe.
>
> Distributed all over world except polar areas. Live near water but not ocean.
> Some shed skin and eat it. Frogs: smooth skin/toads: bumpy skin.
> Hide during daytime (so not eaten by other animals, not too hot). Eat insects.
> Inflate bodies to look larger (scare off other animals).
> Last 30 years numbers smaller: no water/development/pollution/climate change/eaten.

B. Read the test responses on pages 72–73 and the notes on page 81 again. Discuss these questions with a partner.

1. Which parts of the notes did the student use for each question? Put the question number beside the notes she used.

2. Which information in the notes did she not use in her test responses? Put an *X* beside the information she did not use. Why didn't she use this information?

3. How did she select what information to use for each question?

Collaborative Writing

A. Work with a partner. Read the following response to a test item. Discuss what is good and what areas need improvement. Underline any key words in the test question.

Explain why the Galapagos giant tortoises were disappearing.

Their disappearance started hundreds of year ago when European sailors discovered the Galapagos Islands. Today the Islands belong to Ecuador. When the sailors first came, there were hundreds of giant tortoises distributed throughout the Islands. The sailors killed many of them for meat. Similarly, they ate fish that they caught in the ocean. When more sailors came, they brought many animals with them, including donkeys, rats, and goats. The donkeys destroyed many nests where the tortoises laid their eggs annually. The rats selected the eggs and baby tortoises to eat. The tortoises walked very slowly compared to the new animals. The goats turned wild. They ate the plants in the environment that the tortoises usually ate. Fortunately, the Islands had a good source of water. The giant tortoise population declined until nearly all of them had disappeared. The tortoise population will be able to grow again. A group of environmentalists transferred many of the wild goats off of the Islands and released them in another place.

B. Discuss these questions together.

1. Did the student use the test question to write the first sentence? Is the first sentence clear?

2. Which sentences provide the most relevant information to the question? Do any sentences provide information that is not important to the test question?

3. Is the information presented in a logical order?

C. Work with your partner to revise the response. Add a sentence to the beginning of the response. Remove information that is irrelevant to the question. Re-order any sentences to show a logical order. Share your revised response with another pair.

Independent Writing

A. Think about how to respond to the test item *Describe some ways that animals help humans*. First, list several examples that you could write about. Use ideas from what you have learned in books, in classes, or through your own experience.

B. Fill this idea web with ideas for your response.

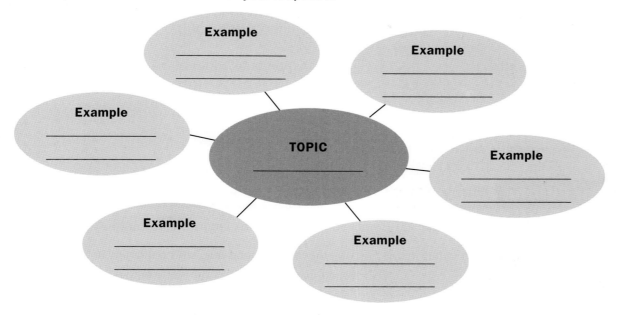

C. Develop a beginning sentence that directly responds to the test question.

D. Decide on a logical sequence for your ideas.

E. Complete these sentences with information that you might want to include.

_____ are an important source of _____

_____.

Scientists use _____ in laboratories to _____

_____.

_____ provide humans with _____

_____.

_____ can be trained to _____

_____.

F. Write your test response. Use your idea web, beginning sentence, and sentences from activity E. In your writing, use the target vocabulary words from page 71 and be sure that your response and examples relate directly to the question.

A. Read your test response. Answer the questions below, and make revisions to your test response as needed.

1. Check (✓) the information you included in your test response.

   ☐ It has a beginning sentence that responds directly to the question.

   ☐ The response relates directly to the question.

   ☐ The information in your response is important to the topic.

   ☐ The information is in a logical sequence.

2. Look at the information you did not include. Would adding that information answer the test question more effectively? Is there any information that you should remove because it is not relevant or important?

Grammar for Editing Many, Much, Fewer, and Less

Count nouns and noncount nouns use different words to describe quantities or amounts.

Use *many*, *few*, and *fewer* with count nouns.

<u>*Many frogs*</u> were hungry.
<u>*Fewer frogs*</u> laid eggs.

Use *much*, *little*, and *less* with noncount nouns.

<u>*Much water*</u> was lost in the hot weather.
<u>*Less water*</u> meant fewer frogs.

B. Check the language in your test response. Revise and edit as needed.

Language Checklist
☐ I used target vocabulary in my test response.
☐ I used count and noncount nouns correctly.
☐ I used *many*, *much*, *fewer*, and *less* correctly.

C. Check your test response again. Repeat activities A and B.

Self-Assessment Review: Go back to page 71 and reassess your knowledge of the target vocabulary. How has your understanding of the words changed? What words do you feel most comfortable using now?

UNIT 7

Are Superstores the Answer?

In this unit, you will

> analyze critical reviews and learn how they are used to compare businesses.
> use comparison/contrast writing.
> increase your understanding of the target academic words for this unit.

WRITING SKILLS

> Comparisons
> Sentence Variety
> **GRAMMAR** Comparative Forms of Adjectives

Self-Assessment

Think about how well you know each target word, and check (✓) the appropriate column. I have…

TARGET WORDS	never seen this word before.	heard or seen the word but am not sure what it means.	heard or seen the word and understand what it means.	used the word confidently in *either* speaking or writing.
AWL				
🔑 alternative				
compute				
🔑 constant				
corporate				
🔑 eliminate				
🔑 emphasis				
🔑 image				
maximize				
🔑 percent				
🔑 volume				

🔑 Oxford 3000™ keywords

Building Knowledge

Read these questions. Discuss your answers in a small group.

1. Are there any "superstores" (very large stores that sell a wide variety of items) near you? If so, describe one.

2. How often do you shop in superstores? What sorts of things do you buy there?

3. What do you like about superstores? What do you dislike about them?

Writing Model

A critical review helps consumers make decisions about where to shop or what to buy. Read a critical review and reader comments from a consumer website.

The Smart Shopper

Shoppers no longer need to go to a shoe store, a furniture store, and then a grocery store. Superstores offer them easier **alternatives**. Thanks to superstores, shoppers can buy shoes, furniture, groceries—and almost everything else—all in one big
5 store.

Superstores all **emphasize** bargain prices. They all have a large selection of merchandise.[1] So what are the differences between these stores? To find out, we took a close look at the two largest stores: BargainBox and SuperMart.

10 **SIZE, SELECTION, AND PRICE**
BargainBox **maximizes** its floor space by making the shopping aisles as narrow as possible. About 30 **percent** of BargainBox's floor space is filled with big appliances such as refrigerators. BargainBox's selection of appliances is bigger than SuperMart's,
15 and its prices are lower.

In contrast, about 30 **percent** of SuperMart's space is filled with clothing. Its clothing is more stylish than BargainBox's. It is also more expensive. SuperMart's clothing brings young people into the store. Its large selection of **computers** and electronics also
20 attracts young people.

---

[1] *merchandise:* things that are for sale

QUALITY AND ENVIRONMENT

Customers also like SuperMart's **image** of high quality. The store is nicely decorated. SuperMart has **eliminated** loud announcements on its sound system. Instead, quiet music plays
25 as shoppers push their carts down the wide aisles. On the other hand, BargainBox is **constantly** packed with shoppers. They hurry up and down the aisles. A large **percentage** of them are parents with children. Parents can leave their children at the large indoor playground while they shop. Moms and dads love this. It makes
30 shopping less stressful for them. However, the playground noise is even louder than the announcements that blare[2] from the sound system at a high **volume**.

Both stores are **maximizing** their profits[3] through a high **volume**
of sales. However, the customers benefit as well. They save time
35 and money. Superstores create a win-win situation.

72 COMMENTS

NEWEST ▼   WRITE A COMMENT

Mom-and-Pop Store
My husband and I own a little grocery store in a small town. Last year, a BargainBox opened up nearby. It stole 80 **percent** of our customers. The goal of **corporations**
40 like BargainBox is to **maximize** profits by **eliminating** competition.[4] It's working. We can't compete with its large selection and low prices. We may have to close our store.
POSTED MAY 28 AT 10:14 A.M.

Money Guy
Who cares if it **maximizes** its **corporate** profits? It also
45 **maximizes** my savings! Shopping at these stores means $$$ in my pockets.
POSTED MAY 28 AT 10:14 A.M.

READ MORE COMMENTS ▼

[2] *blare:* to make a loud, unpleasant noise
[3] *profits:* money that you get when you sell something for more than it cost to buy or make
[4] *competition:* other companies that are trying to achieve the same goals

LEARN

The writer of this review compares two superstores. However, the purpose of the article is not just to show similarities and differences. The review also suggests that each superstore is better than the other one in some ways. In the review, the writer communicates these opinions by choosing words with positive or negative meanings.

When you write a comparison of two places, follow these steps:

- Choose several aspects, features, or parts of the places.

- Write one section about each part of your comparison.

- Show how the two places are similar and different in each section.

- Use a dictionary or thesaurus to find words that show positive and negative opinions.

- Use specific vocabulary. Avoid vague words (*good, bad, nice*).

APPLY

A. Complete this summary of some of the comparisons in the review.

	BargainBox	SuperMart
Size, selection, and price	30% appliances	30% clothing
	_____ selection	more _____
	cheaper	more _____
Quality and environment	very busy	nicely _____
	_____ for children	wide aisles
	noise from _____ and _____	_____ music

B. These words are from the review and from the readers' comments. Write a plus sign (+) beside words that suggest something good or positive. Write a minus sign (–) beside words that suggest something bad or negative. Some words may suggest something both positive and negative.

___ bargain	___ destroy	___ easy	___ expensive	___ family
___ fast	___ great	___ loud	___ nice	___ noisy
___ oversized	___ pleasant	___ profit	___ quality	___ quiet
___ safe	___ save	___ stole	___ stressful	___ stylish

Analyze

A. Complete the chart. Discuss your answers with a partner or small group.

	Positive or negative?	How do you know?	Do you agree?
Writer's opinion of SuperMart			
Writer's opinion of BargainBox			
Mom-and-Pop Store's opinion about BargainBox			

B. The first, second, and sixth paragraphs describe similarities between SuperMart and BargainBox. What are they?

_____

_____

_____

_____

C. Discuss these questions as a class.

1. What information in the review or comments influenced you and your classmates most?

2. How did the language used in the review and in the comments influence your opinions?

Vocabulary Activities   STEP I: Word Level

A. A *corporation* is a big company. The adjective form is *corporate*. Work with a partner. Match phrases on the left with phrases on the right to make complete sentences.

____ 1. Our corporation's profits   a. were higher this year than last year.

____ 2. The corporate growth   b. is a flying bird.

____ 3. The symbol of our corporation   c. are in Malaysia.

____ 4. Our corporate headquarters   d. is in the public safety sector.

B. Match the people with what they *compute*. Work with a partner. Take turns making sentences.

_____ 1. teachers   a. how much a customer owes

_____ 2. sales clerks   b. the speed of a rocket

_____ 3. architects   c. students' test scores

_____ 4. engineers   d. how much a new building will cost

The nouns *percentage* and *percent* are mathematical terms that refer to "one part of every hundred."

Percentage is used with nonspecific numbers.

> A large **percentage** of the customers mentioned the store's playground.

Percent is used with specific numbers. The symbol % is sometimes used instead of the written word.

> About 30 **percent** of the store is filled with appliances.

 CORPUS

C. Look at the chart that shows employee ages at a corporation. Use the chart to complete these sentences using *percentage* or *percent*.

Ages:	18–24	25–34	35–44	45–65	65+
%:	12	24	36	21	7

1. The highest ___*percentage*___ of workers is in the 35–44 age group.
2. What is the _____ of workers under 25?
3. Twenty-one _____ of the workers are between 45 and 65.
4. The lowest _____ of workers is over 65.
5. Nearly 25 _____ of the workers are between 25 and 34.

The word *image* has many different meanings.

An *image* is "the impression that a person or an organization gives to the public."

> SuperMart values **image** over bargains.

An *image* is also "a picture on paper or in a mirror."

> The boy saw his **image** in the store window.

An *image* is also "a picture in people's minds of someone or something."

> I have a funny **image** of you screaming as you run out of a noisy store.

 CORPUS

D. Work with a partner. Match the phrases on the left with the phrases on the right to make complete sentences.

_____ 1. Images of the accident keep me awake at night

_____ 2. I saw my own image

_____ 3. The image on the television screen is not clear

_____ 4. The store's image improved

a. after it was remodeled.

b. because I was very scared.

c. so I can't identify the actor.

d. when I looked in the pond.

Vocabulary Activities STEP II: Sentence Level

To *emphasize* something means "to stress something or to give something importance."

> *The store's advertisements **emphasize** its low prices.*

The noun *emphasis* means "stress or importance given to something." In writing, sometimes use **boldfaced font,** use *italics,* or <u>underline a word</u> to give it *emphasis.*

> *They also place **emphasis** on the store's friendly workers.*

The word *emphatic* means "saying or expressing something in a strong way."

> *My wife **was emphatic**. She said, "No! I won't shop there."*

> *She told me **emphatically**, "I hate that store!"*

CORPUS

E. Rewrite each sentence using the words in parentheses. Compare your sentences with a partner.

A salesperson from an advertising agency met with the owner of a new café. They discussed how to advertise the café.

1. The salesperson said the ad should stress what is special about the café. (emphasize)

   The salesperson said the ad should emphasize what is special about the café.

2. She suggested that the importance should be on the café's excellent location. (emphasis)

   _____

3. The owner said strongly that the stress should be on the food. (emphatically, emphasis)

   _____

4. The owner's strong words convinced the salesperson to stress the food's quality. (emphatic, emphasize)

   _____

F. An *alternative* is "a thing that you can choose instead of something else." The adjective form is also *alternative*. Imagine that several people are discussing how to arrange the floor space in a new superstore. Rewrite the sentences using the word in parentheses. Compare your sentences with a partner.

1. There are several possible locations for the sports department. (alternative)

   There are several alternative locations for the sports department.

2. One choice is to put it near the rear door. (alternative)

   _____

3. Or, instead, we could put it next to the shoe department. (alternatively)

   _____

4. Neither of those choices appeals to me. (alternatives)

   _____

5. Do you have a different plan? (alternative)

   _____

The noun *volume* can be count or noncount.

As a count noun, *volume* refers to "a book, often one in a set of books."

> *This dictionary has three **volumes**.*

As a noncount noun, *volume* refers to "the loudness of sound." *High volume* is loud. *Low volume* is quiet. To ask for a louder sound, we say, "Turn up the volume." To ask for a softer sound, we say, "Turn down the volume."

> *Please turn up the **volume** on the television. I can't hear it.*

Volume as a noncount and count noun also refers to "the amount of something." In this case, we can use the words *high, large, huge,* or *low* to describe the volume.

> *Look at the huge **volume** of mail we received today.*

CORPUS

G. Answer the following questions using the word *volume* in your answer.

1. What types of books often come in volumes?

   _____

2. In which situations would you want to listen to sound at a high volume? In which situations would you want to listen to sound at a low volume?

   _____

3. What types of things do superstores have a large volume of?

   _____

The verb to *maximize* means "to increase something as much as possible."

*We can **maximize** our store hours by opening early in the morning.*

The word *maximum* is both a noun and an adjective. It refers to "the greatest amount of something that is possible."

*This theater can seat a **maximum** of 520 people.*

*The **maximum** seating in this theater is 520.*

CORPUS

H. Imagine that you are the owner of a restaurant. It is very small, and you want to be able to seat more customers. Write two sentences that describe how you could *maximize* the restaurant's seating space. Use *maximize* or *maximum* in your sentences. Share your sentences with a partner.

1. *The restaurant seats a maximum of 20 people.*

2. _____

3. _____

I. The adjective *constant* refers to something that "happens all the time." Write three sentences that describe a busy superstore. Include a form of *constant* in each sentence.

1. *New customers are constantly coming in.*

2. _____

3. _____

4. _____

J. To *eliminate* something means to "get rid of it." With a partner, check all of the items you want to *eliminate* from a restaurant that you just bought. Then take turns making sentences with the underlined words.

| broken chairs | flies | kitchen | mice |
| doors | food | ✓ lazy waiters | restrooms |

I want to eliminate lazy waiters because they slow orders down.

_____

_____

_____

_____

_____

Grammar | Comparative Forms of Adjectives

Comparative adjectives describe the differences between two or more similar items. There are several ways to form comparative adjectives.

For one-syllable words, add *-er* to the adjective. If the word ends in *-e*, just add *-r*.

fast	→	faster	safe	→	safer
cheap	→	cheaper	wide	→	wider

Do not add an ending to adjectives with two or more syllables. Instead, put *more* or *less* in front of the adjective.

expensive	→	more expensive	→	less expensive
helpful	→	more helpful	→	less helpful

To compare two things, use *than* after the comparative form of the adjective.

BargainBox is more crowded <u>*than*</u> SuperMart.

Some adjectives have special forms for comparison.

good	→	better	bad	→	worse

A. With a partner, look back at the writing model on pages 86–87. Underline words and phrases that compare.

B. Complete the charts with the missing forms of each adjective.

Adjective	Comparative
nice	nicer
expensive	
	nearer
fast	

Adjective	Comparative
low	
small	
pleasant	
	larger

C. Answer the questions using comparative forms of adjectives. Compare your answers with a partner.

1. How do prices in superstores compare with prices in traditional stores?

_____

2. How does the clothing at SuperMart compare with the clothing at BargainBox?

_____

3. Which store do you think will be more successful? Why?

_____

WRITING SKILL Sentence Variety

LEARN

Usually there are several ways to express the same idea. Good writers try to vary the patterns of their sentences. This makes their writing more interesting to read. A different sentence pattern can also help writers express ideas more clearly.

Here are some ways to vary sentences:

- Word order

  A common sentence pattern begins with *there is* or *there are*. You can often omit these words and change the position of the information.

  There is a flower shop next to the restaurant.
  A flower shop is next to the restaurant.

- Prepositional phrases

  Place prepositional phrases in different positions.

  The store is crowded on Mondays.
  On Mondays, the store is crowded.

- Combining sentences

  Sometimes you can combine two or more simple sentences into one sentence.

  The restaurant is large. The restaurant is located in a mall.
  The large restaurant is located in a mall.

APPLY

Read the review of the superstores again and discuss the following questions with a partner.

1. Many sentences compare BargainBox and SuperMart. Find two different sentence patterns that the author uses to make the comparisons.

2. How does the author present the following ideas to make them less repetitive?

   BargainBox is maximizing its profits through a high volume of sales. SuperMart is also maximizing its profits through a high volume of sales.

3. Find one sentence that combines the following ideas.

   Quiet music plays. Shoppers push their carts down aisles. The aisles are wide.

Collaborative Writing

A. The review on pages 86–87 does not mention what the BargainBox store looks like except that it is big and has narrow aisles. Work with a partner. Discuss what you think the store looks like. Then write two sentences that describe the inside of the store. Try to use the same style of writing that is used in the rest of the review.

_____

_____

B. With the same partner, write two more sentences to describe the inside of SuperMart. Compare the two stores in your sentences.

_____

_____

C. Look over your sentences together. Do they include a variety of sentence types? Do they sound like the sentences in the review?

D. Share your sentences with the class. Discuss these questions.

1. How does the writing style compare with the style used in the original review?

2. Would the addition of this new information improve the review? Why, or why not?

Independent Writing

A. Choose two restaurants that you want to compare in a review for a consumer magazine. You can choose restaurants that you have been to, or you can create imaginary restaurants. Name your restaurants.

_____

B. Look at the list of features below. Check (✓) the three that you want to write about.

_____ food _____ service _____ environment

_____ cleanliness _____ location _____ price

> **VOCABULARY TIP**
>
> You will need adjectives to describe and compare the two restaurants. Use a dictionary or thesaurus to find appropriate words. For example, some good adjectives for comparing food are *tasty, delicious*, and *flavorful*.

C. Organize the information. Write about the least important feature first, and finish with the most important feature, so it will be what the reader remembers best.

1. _____

2. _____

3. _____

D. Choose adjectives to describe the restaurants. Sort your adjectives into positive or negative words. Also, look up their comparative forms.

Positive	Negative	Comparative
tasty	tasteless	tastier
		more tasteless

E. Complete these sentences with information that you might include in the review.

1. The _____ was especially _____ at _____.

2. _____ cover the walls.

3. The waiters seemed _____.

4. Best of all, this restaurant _____.

5. Compared to _____, this restaurant is _____.

6. _____ was the best dish, but it was _____.

7. Each table in _____ had _____.

8. It was so _____ in the restaurant that _____.

F. Write your restaurant review. Compare each restaurant using the same features. Use effective adjectives that clearly express your ideas and opinions. In your writing, use the target vocabulary words from page 85 and include a variety of sentence structures.

A. Read your review. Answer the questions below, and make revisions to your review as needed.

1. Check (✓) the information you included in your review.

   ☐ an introduction that tells readers which restaurants you are reviewing

   ☐ a comparison of the two restaurant based on three features

   ☐ both negative and positive words to describe each restaurant

2. Look at the information you did not include. Would adding that information make your review more complete?

Grammar for Editing | Subject-Verb Agreement

The subject in a sentence tells who or what the sentence is about. The subject of a sentence can be singular or plural. It is important that the verb in a sentence agrees with the subject.

If the subject is singular, use the singular form of the verb. If the subject is plural, use the plural form of the verb.

> S   V   S   V
> The *food* *tastes* delicious. / The *lights* *are* soft.

The plurals of most count nouns are formed by adding *–s* or *–ies* to the noun.

| store → stores | price → prices | baby → babies |

Some plurals are irregular and do not end in *–s*:

| child → children | person → people | woman → women |

B. Check the language in your review. Revise and edit as needed.

Language Checklist
☐ I used target words in my review.
☐ I used descriptive adjectives.
☐ I used comparative forms of adjectives correctly.
☐ I used correct subject-verb agreement.

C. Check your review again. Repeat activities A and B.

Self-Assessment Review: Go back to page 85 and reassess your knowledge of the target vocabulary. How has your understanding of the words changed? What words do you feel more comfortable using now?

Understanding Brain Injuries

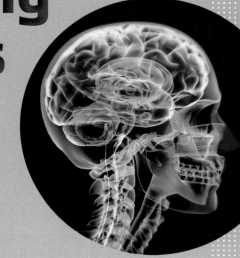

In this unit, you will

> analyze informational brochures and learn how they are used to inform people about neuroscience.
> use informational writing.
> increase your understanding of the target academic words for this unit.

WRITING SKILLS

> Analyzing Audience
> Organizing Information
> **GRAMMAR** Real Conditionals

Self-Assessment

Think about how well you know each target word, and check (✓) the appropriate column. I have…

TARGET WORDS	never seen this word before.	heard or seen the word but am not sure what it means.	heard or seen the word and understand what it means.	used the word confidently in *either* speaking or writing.
AWL				
evaluate				
exceed				
🔑 fundamental				
guideline				
🔑 institute				
minimal				
🔑 minimum				
🔑 professional				
🔑 revise				
🔑 transport				

🔑 Oxford 3000™ keywords

Building Knowledge

Read these questions. Discuss your answers in a small group.

1. What do you know about brain injuries?

2. Have you ever heard about athletes having brain injuries?

3. What problems do people face if they have damage to their brains?

Writing Models

Informational brochures about health are often found in hospitals or distributed to specific people who need to know the information. Read two brochures about brain injury.

Understanding TBI

Traumatic brain injury (TBI) is a serious medical condition. TBI can lead to disabilities[1] and even death. It is important for patients and their families to be aware of this condition, its causes, and its signs.

CAUSES OF BRAIN INJURY

5 Traumatic brain injury results from a hard hit to the head. TBIs most often happen while people are working, riding in a vehicle, or playing sports.

SIGNS OF BRAIN INJURY

People with TBI may be confused or forget things. They may faint, vomit, or have a headache. They may feel dizzy[2] or not see clearly. There may be
10 obvious changes in their speech, mood, or body movements.

SEVERITY AND TREATMENT FOR TBI

A person with signs of brain injury should get immediate medical care. A medical **professional** will use an electronic brain scan to rate the injury as mild, moderate, or severe.

15 • About 80 percent of TBIs are mild. Most people with mild TBI are completely well within three weeks with a **minimum** of problems. They have **minimal** brain damage and need no special treatment.

• About ten percent of TBIs are moderate. People with moderate TBIs often need treatment for physical or mental problems.

20 • The ten percent who **exceed** the moderate rating may have lifelong problems, even after surgery. ■

---

[1] *disability:* loss of some or total ability to use a part of the body
[2] *dizzy:* a feeling that everything is turning around and that you are going to fall

Concussions in Sports

Brain concussions happen to athletes every day. Coaches in all sports should know the signs of a concussion and respond quickly. Your job as coach is to strengthen your players. You
5 must also protect them.

WHICH SPORTS ARE THE MOST DANGEROUS?
Concussions happen in nearly every sport. They are most common in rough sports such as football, soccer, hockey, boxing, and rugby.

10 ### WHAT SHOULD YOU DO IF A PLAYER IS INJURED?
The **fundamental** rule is to remove a player from the game immediately. Even if a player says, "I'm OK, Coach," take him or her out of the game and **evaluate** his or her condition. If you think a player has a concussion, immediately call an ambulance to **transport** the player to a hospital.

15 ### WHAT ARE THE SIGNS OF CONCUSSION?
Athletes are tough. They often try to hide their injuries. It's up to you[1] to read the warning signs. Train teammates and parents to watch for the signs, too.
Players with a concussion may
- be confused
20 - forget instructions
- feel dizzy or lose their balance
- speak slowly or unclearly
- vomit, faint, or have a headache
- behave or move in an odd way

25 ### WHAT CAN YOU DO TO PREVENT CONCUSSIONS?
It's impossible to prevent all concussions. However, coaches can follow these **guidelines** to reduce the number of concussions:
1. **Institute** rules that require all players to wear protective equipment.
2. Don't let players become too tired. Tired players react slowly and may
30 take dangerous chances.
3. **Revise** game rules. For example, don't permit sliding in baseball. ■

---

[1] *It's up to you:* It is your responsibility.

LEARN

Informational brochures are usually written for a specific audience (group of readers). Writers choose what information to include, what language to use, and how to organize the information based on this audience. For example, technical or medical language would be appropriate for nurses, but it might not be appropriate for soccer players.

Before you write an informational brochure, ask yourself these questions:

1. Who will read the brochure?
2. What information does the audience need?
3. How much does the audience probably already know about the topic?
4. How will the audience affect the language and structure of the brochure?

APPLY

Fill in the chart with information about each brochure. Compare your notes with a partner.

	Pamphlet 1	Pamphlet 2
Who is the most likely audience?	☐ doctors ☐ patients ☐ workers	☐ nurses ☐ athletes ☐ coaches
What information does this audience need?		
Does the brochure use technical language? If so, what?		
Does the author write directly to the reader using the pronoun *you*?	☐ yes ☐ no	☐ yes ☐ no
How does the author introduce each section of the brochure?	☐ a phrase ☐ a question	☐ a phrase ☐ a question

Analyze

A. What extra information might each group of people want from the "Concussions in Sports" brochure? Check (✓) the boxes. Then discuss your answers with a partner.

Information	Medical students	Athletes
1. The technical names for different types of concussion	☐	☐
2. The effect of concussion on the brain, spine, and nerves	☐	☐
3. How the signs of concussion change in the weeks after an injury	☐	☐
4. How to avoid brain injuries when playing sports	☐	☐
5. Advice for talking to a coach about concussions	☐	☐
6. Types of tests and scans that doctors can do after a concussion	☐	☐
7. How to do brain surgery on people with concussions	☐	☐

B. What effect do these text choices have? Match the answers. You can use the same effect more than once. Discuss your answers with a partner. Can you think of other effects of these choices?

_____ 1. Using *you*

_____ 2. Asking and answering questions

_____ 3. Using technical words

_____ 4. Using abbreviations (*TBI*)

_____ 5. Including statistics (*80 percent*)

_____ 6. Writing in the imperative

    (*Look carefully…*)

a. gives readers enough information to talk to their doctors.

b. shows readers that they need to know this information.

c. helps readers find the most important information.

d. makes the information appear serious but not too worrying.

e. saves space and avoids repetition.

A. To *exceed* means "to go beyond or above something." Complete the sentences with *exceed/exceeds* or *don't/doesn't exceed*.

1. Applicants for the job must be over 18. Jack is 22. Jack _____*exceeds*_____ the minimum age requirement.

2. The bridge can support cars and trucks up to 3,000 kilograms. That truck weighs 2,800 kilograms. It _____ the maximum weight requirement.

3. A basketball team can have five players. That team has seven! It _____ the maximum number of players allowed.

4. On my new diet, I can eat 1,500 calories a day. I've already had about 1,450, so I won't have dessert. I don't want to _____ my calorie allowance for today.

5. Be careful! _____ the speed limit! You're already driving very fast.

6. If you want to stay healthy, cut down on the amount of sugar and fat you eat. You should not _____ the amounts that doctors recommend.

B. Work with a partner. Complete the paragraph with words from the box. Take turns reading the completed paragraph.

revise	evaluates	institute	transports	guidelines

When someone reports a medical emergency, an ambulance rushes to the scene. An emergency medical technician (EMT) quickly _____
(1. forms an opinion about)
the patient's condition. The EMT follows the _____ set by doctors.
(2. rules)
First, the EMT checks the patient's breathing. Then she checks the patient's heartbeat. The EMT will _____ life-saving procedures if the patient
(3. start)
stops breathing or if the patient's heart stops. The EMT must be ready to
_____ the treatment if the patient does not respond. If the patient's
(4. change)
condition is serious, the EMT continues the emergency treatment while the
ambulance _____ the patient to a hospital.
(5. moves)

If something is *fundamental*, it is "the most important" or "the most basic."

> A **fundamental** rule is to remove players who are hit in the head.

If two things are *fundamentally* different, the differences are at a very basic level.

> There are **fundamental** differences between traumatic brain injury (TBI) and acquired brain injury (ABI). TBI is caused by injuries to the head, while ABI is caused by tumors or infections.

> Traumatic brain injuries and acquired brain injuries are **fundamentally** different.

 CORPUS

C. Explain how the following items are *fundamentally* different.

1. night and day

   A fundamental difference is that it is dark at night and it is light during the day.

2. doctors and dentists

   _____

3. motorcycles and bicycles

   _____

4. basketball and soccer

   _____

The noun *institution* refers to "a big organization such as a bank, hospital, prison, or school."

> Many health care **institutions** specialize in caring for TBI patients.

> Many financial **institutions** offer school loans.

To *institutionalize* means "to enroll someone in a hospital."

> My uncle's family **institutionalized** him because he had severe brain damage.

The verb *institute* means "to organize or start something."

> The hospital **instituted** a special program for TBI patients.

 CORPUS

D. Rewrite each sentence to include the form of *institute* in parentheses. Share your new sentences with a partner.

1. The thief was put in a prison as punishment for his crimes. (institutionalized)

   The thief was institutionalized as punishment for his crimes.

2. Our company started a program to find talented scientists. (instituted)

   _____

3. The hospital tries to make living there feel like living at home. (institution)

   _____

4. Next year, I hope to attend a nursing school. (institute)

   _____

E. To *evaluate* something means "to form an opinion about something after thinking about it carefully." Write sentences to describe what the following people *evaluate*.

1. a doctor *A doctor evaluates a patient's health.* _____

2. a professor _____

3. a tennis coach _____

4. a store owner _____

F. When you *revise* something, you change it to make it better or more correct. What do the following people *revise* as part of their daily work?

1. a newspaper editor _____

2. a software engineer _____

3. a chef _____

4. a soccer coach _____

A *professional* is "a person who works in a job that needs a lot of studying, skill, and special training."

> *We publish books to help medical **professionals** become more successful.*

The same word is used as an adjective.

> *My mother is a **professional** counselor.*

> *The student's website was neat, easy to use, and very **professional**.*

An athlete who is paid to play sports is called a *professional player*, or *pro*.

> ***Professional** tennis players compete each year at Wimbledon.*

> *Only **pros** can compete there.*

CORPUS

G. Rewrite each sentence using the word *professional*. Compare your sentences with a partner.

1. Muhammad Ali was paid for boxing.

   Muhammad Ali was a professional boxer.

2. Be sure to dress like a businessperson when you go to a job interview.

   _____

3. The hospital hired three new people who are trained in medical care.

   _____

The root word *mini* means "small." The root *maxi* means "big." Many words in English have these roots.

A *minimum* is "the smallest amount possible." *Maximum* refers to "the biggest amount possible."

> TBI patients should rest for a **minimum** of three weeks.
>
> After three weeks, they can exercise for a **maximum** of one hour daily.

Note that the words *minimum* and *maximum* are often followed by the preposition *of* and words that give an amount.

The adjective *minimal* describes a very small amount.

> Even patients with **minimal** brain damage should avoid too much exercise.

CORPUS

H. Write sentences to answer the following questions. Use *minimum* or *minimal*.

1. People often say, "Bigger is better." In which situations is it better to have a minimal amount of something?

   _____

   _____

2. What is the minimum number of years a person should attend school?

   _____

   _____

Grammar Real Conditionals

Present real conditional sentences express a result of something that happens regularly or is generally true.

When clause	Result clause	Example
simple present	simple present	*When it rains, the sidewalks get wet.*

Every time that it rains, the sidewalks get wet.

Future real conditional sentences express the possibility that something will occur in the future.

Result clause	If- clause	Example
will	simple present	*I will stay home if it rains.*

It is not raining now. However, the writer plans to stay home if it rains later.

Often the result clause includes a modal (*will, should, can*).

If- clause	Result clause	Example
simple present	will	*If I feel better, I will go with you.*
	should	*If you feel sick, you should stay home.*

When you are giving advice or directions, you don't need the word *will*.

If- clause	Result clause	Example
simple present	imperative	*If you need more medicine, let me know.*
		Let me know if you need more medicine.

The *if-* or *when-* clause can go at the beginning or the end of a sentence. The meaning does not change. However, when the *if-* or *when-* clause is at the beginning of the sentence, it is followed by a comma.

A. Underline the *if-* or *when-* clause. Circle the result clause.

1. If a person receives a bump on the head, watch her closely.

2. A person may need surgery if he has a serious brain injury.

3. A professional should evaluate the case if a person shows signs of TBI.

4. When you play without a helmet, you are likely to get injured.

B. Complete each sentence with your own ideas.

1. If I don't get enough exercise, _____.

2. When people don't follow guidelines, _____.

3. Your writing will be much better if you _____.

4. You can save money if you _____.

5. If you want to become a professional athlete, _____.

WRITING SKILL Organizing Information

LEARN

Space in a brochure is limited, and the topic is often complex. To make the information easy for readers to understand, writers organize the information carefully. Writers use the following strategies:

- Group information into topics in separate paragraphs.
- Use headings to tell readers what each paragraph will be about.
- List important ideas with bullet points (•) or numbers.

APPLY

A. Work in a small group. Review the brochure on page 100. Then discuss the questions below.

1. How does the writer divide the information?

2. What headings does the author use?

3. What is the topic of each section?

4. Why did the writer choose this order?

5. Does the writer use bulleted lists or numbered lists?

B. Review the brochure on page 101 with your group. Discuss these questions.

1. How does the writer divide the information?

2. What is the topic of each section?

3. How do the headings in this brochure differ from those in the first brochure?

4. Both brochures have a section on the signs of the condition. Which one is easier to read? Why?

Collaborative Writing

A. Work as a class. The second brochure does not include a definition of a concussion. Plan a section that will describe what a concussion is. Answer the following questions.

1. What will your heading say?

2. Where will you include this information? Why?

B. Use the information below to write your paragraph for the brochure. Have your teacher or a volunteer write your new paragraph on the board.

Concussion:	A type of traumatic brain injury
How athletes get concussions:	Fall down Hit head Hit by another player Head moves suddenly and violently Brain moves within the skull
Seriousness:	Can cause minimal damage Can be severe and cause lifelong problems

C. Evaluate and revise your paragraph.

1. Is the information presented in a logical order?

2. Does the style of your heading match the other headings?

3. Does your language sound like the rest of the brochure?

4. Will coaches understand your paragraph?

D. Revise the paragraph together. Then read the whole brochure to be sure it will be useful to coaches.

Independent Writing

A. Think about what information to include in a brochure for parents of children ages 6–12 about concussions.

Choose headings for your brochure. Make notes in the chart about what information you want to include. Check the brochure on page 101 and the information on page 110 for ideas, but remember you're writing for a different audience.

Heading	Information

B. Write a short introduction that explains why the information is useful to parents.

C. Complete these sentences with information that you might want to include.

The first sign of _____ is _____.

Your child may feel _____.

Take your child to _____ for an evaluation.

In the first few days, _____.

Be sure that your child _____.

Don't allow your child to _____.

D. Write a title for your brochure.

E. Write the text of your brochure. Think about your audience and include appropriate information. In your writing, use the target vocabulary words from page 99 and include the headings, introduction, and sentences from activities B, C, and D.

A. Read your informational brochure. Answer the questions below, and make revisions to your brochure as needed.

1. Check (✓) the information you included in your brochure.

   ☐ an introduction that tells why the information is important for parents
   ☐ facts and information that will help parents understand the condition
   ☐ clearly worded headings for each group of facts

2. Look at the information you did not include. Would adding that information make your brochure more complete and understandable to your audience?

Grammar for Editing Punctuating Lists

If a list is introduced by an incomplete sentence, don't use capital letters after the bullets. Use end punctuation if each item completes the stem.

Players with concussions may

- be confused.
- feel dizzy.

If a list is introduced by a complete sentence with a colon, use capital letters after the bullets when the bulleted information is not in complete sentences. Do not use end punctuation.

Players with concussions may have these symptoms:

- Confusion
- Dizziness

If the information after the bullets or numbers is a complete sentence, then capitalize the first letter and use end punctuation.

Players with concussions could have these symptoms:

1. They might appear confused.
2. They could feel dizzy.

B. Check the language in your brochure. Revise and edit as needed.

Language Checklist
☐ I used target vocabulary words in my pamphlet.
☐ I used conditional sentences correctly.
☐ I punctuated bulleted and numbered lists correctly.

C. Check your brochure again. Repeat activities A and B.

Self-Assessment Review: Go back to page 99 and reassess your knowledge of the target vocabulary. How has your understanding of the words changed? What words do you feel most comfortable using now?

9

Our Thirst for Water

In this unit, you will

> analyze a scientific article and learn how it is used to inform people about oceanography.
> use process writing.
> increase your understanding of the target academic words for this unit.

WRITING SKILLS

> Describing a Process
> Academic Language
> **GRAMMAR** Words That Signal a Contrast

Self-Assessment

Think about how well you know each target word, and check (✓) the appropriate column. I have…

TARGET WORDS	never seen this word before.	heard or seen the word but am not sure what it means.	heard or seen the word and understand what it means.	used the word confidently in *either* speaking or writing.
AWL				
🔑 analyze				
🔑 convince				
🔑 decade				
🔑 foundation				
journal				
🔑 option				
🔑 quote				
specify				
🔑 theme				
🔑 version				

🔑 Oxford 3000™ keywords

113

Building Knowledge

Read these questions. Discuss your answers in a small group.

1. Why do people need water?

2. Where does the water supply in your home city come from?

3. What are some sources of water?

Writing Model

Scientific articles often appear in scientific journals or magazines. Read this article about a process for removing salt from sea water.

Desalination: Getting the Salt Out

"Today we have energy wars. Tomorrow it will be water wars," says water **analyst** Erik Harmon. This warning seems odd. After all, 71
5 percent of Earth is covered by water. So, how is it that people complain, "We are surrounded by water, but we are thirsty"?

The facts explain the **quotation**:

10 • 97 percent of Earth's water is salt water.

• 780 million people on Earth do not have easy access to safe drinking water.

15 • By 2030, 47 percent of the people on Earth will live in places with water shortages.[1]

Desalination plants make salt water safe for drinking.

Climate changes over the last **decade** have dried up many traditional sources of water. Without water, the world faces serious economic and health problems. The **theme** is the same around the world: *We cannot live without water.*

20 Scientists have a possible solution: desalination plants. These factories remove salt from ocean water. The process could provide a continuous supply of pure water. "It could save lives," an editorial on desalination says. The argument is **convincing**.

Many countries in the Middle East and North Africa already have desalination
25 plants. Other countries have plans to build desalination plants.

―――――――――――
[1] *water shortage:* a situation where there is not enough water

BUILDING DESALINATION PLANTS

The first step in building a desalination plant is to find a good location. Engineers evaluate possible sites to find the best one. Then they **analyze** the country's water needs. They consider alternative **versions** of desalination systems. They compute the amount of salt-free water that each system will generate. Finally, the engineers
30 **specify** which system they think is best.

SOLAR-POWERED SYSTEMS

There are several types of desalination systems. One type uses the sun for energy. This solar-powered system consists of sealed chambers.[2] The roof of each
35 chamber is made of glass. The **foundation** is a shallow tub.[3] First, a pump[4] fills the tub with sea water. Sunlight passes through the glass roof to heat the water. Then steam from the hot water rises. As the steam
40 cools, drops of water form on the inside of the glass roof. The drops are salt-free. Soon the drops roll down and fall into a pipe. Finally, the pipe delivers fresh water to homes, factories, and farms.

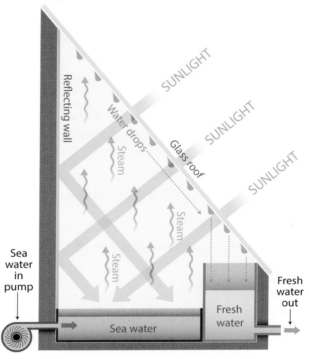

A solar-powered desalination system uses energy from the sun.

ADVANTAGES OF SOLAR-POWERED SYSTEMS

45 A solar-powered system has several advantages over other systems. First, a solar-powered system uses free energy from the sun. In contrast, other systems use expensive coal, oil, or nuclear energy. Second, while other systems require expensive machinery, solar systems do not.
50 In addition, a solar-powered system is easy to use and maintain, whereas other systems need highly trained professionals to do these tasks. However, a solar-powered system has one serious problem. It will work only in locations where the sun shines many hours a day all year long.

Unfortunately, desalination is not an **option** for countries far from an ocean.
55 These countries must use other solutions, such as recycling water. (For information on wastewater[5] recycling, see the March edition of *The Water Journal*.)

---

[2] *sealed chamber:* a tightly enclosed space
[3] *shallow tub:* a container for liquids that is not deep
[4] *pump:* a machine that moves liquid
[5] *wastewater:* dirty water that has already been used for cleaning, manufacturing, etc.

LEARN

Scientific writing often describes processes. A process is the ways things work or the stages in a sequence of events. The description of a process needs to be very clearly organized. For example, scientists usually describe their experiments and techniques in detail so that other scientists can do the experiments for themselves. Therefore, when you describe a process, you will often include transitions and other time signal words such as these:

first	first	the first step	the first stage
second	then	the second step	the next stage
third	finally	the last step	the final stage

When you describe a process, follow these steps:

- Give the name and purpose of the process.
- List all the stages in the correct order.
- Use transition words and time markers to show the sequence.

APPLY

A. Reread the sixth paragraph. Circle transition words. Complete the outline.

Process: Building Desalination Plants

1. *Find a good location* _____
2. _____
3. _____
4. _____
5. _____
6. _____

B. Reread the seventh paragraph. Circle transition words and time markers. Complete the outline.

Process: Solar-Powered Desalination System

1. *Pump fills the tub with sea water* _____
2. _____
3. _____
4. _____
5. _____

Analyze

A. Choose the best answer for each question.

1. What is the purpose of the first five paragraphs of the article?

   a. To describe the process of desalination

   b. To show the need for desalination

   c. To explain a problem with desalination

2. What is the purpose of the last section ("Advantages of Solar-Powered Systems")?

   a. To explain which countries can and cannot use solar-powered systems

   b. To introduce different types of desalination plants

   c. To explain why solar-powered systems are better than other types of systems

3. Which verb tense does the writer use to describe the processes?

   a. Simple present

   b. Simple past

   c. Present perfect

B. Discuss these questions with a partner.

1. Did you find the introduction to the article interesting? Why, or why not?

   _____

   _____

2. Why does the writer use headings for each section of the article?

   _____

   _____

3. Who do you think reads articles like this one?

   _____

   _____

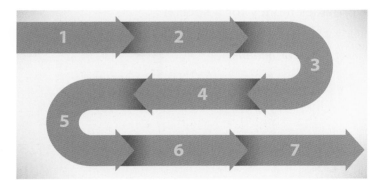

Both the word *decade* and the word *version* are nouns.

A *decade* is "a time period of ten years."

   *Many new technologies were developed in the last **decade**.*

A *version* of something is slightly different from another similar item.

   *As technology improves, companies create new **versions** of cell phones.*

   *One **version** of a desalination plant uses solar power.*

A. Work with a partner. Complete the paragraph using the correct forms of *decade* and *version*.

Over a century ago, a ship named *The Titanic* hit an iceberg in the North

Atlantic Ocean. The ship sank in a terrible tragedy. Two (1) _____

of the tragedy have been made into movies. One (2) _____ was

made four (3) _____ after the event. That (4) _____

told the story of a family. A second movie was made about two

(5) _____ ago, in 1997. The second (6) _____ was

about a young couple.

The noun *foundation* has several different meanings.

One meaning refers to "the bricks or stones that form the solid base of a building under the ground."

   *A storm knocked down the lighthouse, and only the **foundation** was left.*

A *foundation* can also be "an idea or fact on which something is based."

   *Hard work is the **foundation** of a successful career in oceanography.*

A *foundation* can also be "an organization that provides money for a special purpose."

   *The World Ocean **Foundation** is raising money to clean up our oceans.*

B. Match the beginning of each sentence to the correct ending. Then discuss which meaning of *foundation* is used in the sentence.

____ 1. After workers built the foundation,

____ 2. The foundation raised money

____ 3. Foundations for sea walls

____ 4. Good language skills form a strong foundation

a. go deep into the ground.

b. they started building the walls.

c. for academic success.

d. to save sea turtles.

C. Match the name of each journal with the theme of its articles.

____ 1. *The Pure Water Journal*

____ 2. *The Journal of Ocean Life*

____ 3. *The Undersea Journal*

____ 4. *The Journal of Ocean Resources*

a. desalination

b. mapping the ocean floor

c. medicines from the sea

d. whales and other sea animals

Vocabulary Activities | STEP II: Sentence Level

Word Form Chart			
Noun	**Verb**	**Adjective**	**Adverb**
analysis analyst	analyze	analytical	analytically

D. Rewrite each sentence to include the word in parentheses. Compare your sentences with those of a partner.

1. A scientist made a study of the behavior of walruses. (analyzed)

   A scientist analyzed the behavior of walruses.

2. The scientist watched walruses carefully to learn about their behavior. (analytically)

   _____

3. The careful study showed that walruses keep their heads above water when they sleep. (analytical)

   _____

4. The study also showed that walruses change color when they come onto land. (analysis)

   _____

5. The person who made the study found that walruses use their teeth to help them walk. (analyst)

   _____

When you *specify* something, you "say it clearly or in detail." The word *specify* is often used in business communications. It is often followed by a clause that begins with *who, what, when, where, why,* or *how.* It can also be followed by an object.

> The engineers **specified** which system they preferred.

> They **specified** where to build the plant.

> They also **specified** the cost of materials and labor.

To *convince* means "to make a person believe or do something."

> The farmers tried to **convince** the government to provide more water.

The words *to, that,* or *of* after *convince* begin a description of what the person should believe or do.

> The writer wants to **convince** readers **that** solar desalination systems are the best option.

> The desalination company **convinced** the government **to** build a desalination plant.

> The government could not **convince** citizens **of** the need for such an expensive plant.

When a person is completely sure of something or has been influenced to believe something, we say the person is *convinced.* When an argument is good and logical, we say it is *convincing.*

> Citizens were not **convinced.**

> The government's reasons were not very **convincing.**

CORPUS

E. Rewrite the paragraph using appropriate forms of *specify* and *convince.* Use the underlined words and phrases for clues.

Yesterday Mayor Boaz spoke at a city council meeting. He tried <u>to tell city leaders</u> to spend money on a desalination plant. He tried <u>to make everyone believe that</u> the city doesn't have enough drinking water. City leaders asked a lot of questions. They wanted the mayor <u>to tell them exactly</u> how much the plant would cost. They wanted Mayor Boaz <u>to tell them just</u> how long the project would take. Mayor Boaz couldn't answer their questions. His argument was <u>not very strong</u>. In the end, city leaders <u>were not influenced</u> to spend the money.

Yesterday Mayor Boaz spoke at a city council meeting. He tried to convince city

leaders to spend money on a desalination plant.

_____

_____

_____

_____

_____

F. An *option* is a choice. If something is *optional*, you can choose it or not choose it. Write three sentences that describe *options* people have to save water. Each sentence should include *option* or *optional*. Compare your sentences with a partner.

1. *Not serving water in restaurants is one option.* _____

2. _____

3. _____

4. _____

A *quotation* consists of the exact words that you repeat from what another person said or wrote. The informal form of the noun *quotation* is *quote*. The verb form is also *quote*.

> Jin included a **quotation** from Coleridge.
> Jin **quoted** Samuel Coleridge.

When you *quote* someone, put *quotation marks* (" ") around the quote.

> A famous **quote** from the British poet Samuel Coleridge is: "Water, water, everywhere / Nor any a drop to drink."

A *quote* can also be a statement of how much a product or service will cost.

> I got a **quote** of $300 from a mechanic to fix my boat.

CORPUS

G. Rewrite the numbered sentences to include a form of *quote*. Compare your sentences with a partner.

I wanted to learn how to scuba dive, so I visited a diving school. (1) A teacher there gave me a price of $900. I was surprised. "That's expensive!" I said. (2) The teacher responded with a famous saying, "You get what you pay for." I asked what the lessons included. She explained that there were six lessons. The first three lessons were in a pool. The last three were in the ocean. (3) I asked if her price included equipment. She laughed. "Of course," she said. "It includes everything, even dry towels."

1. *A teacher there quoted a price of $900.* _____

2. _____

3. _____

Grammar Words That Signal a Contrast

You can use many different words to show contrast.

The conjunction *but* shows contrast in a compound sentence.

The world is covered with water, <u>*but*</u> most of it is salt water.

The words *whereas* and *while* show contrast in different clauses of a sentence. *Whereas* is more formal than *while*.

A solar-powered system is easy to use, <u>*whereas*</u> other systems need highly trained professionals.

Other systems require expensive machinery, <u>*while*</u> solar systems do not.

You can also use transitions such as *however* and *in contrast*.

A solar-powered system uses energy from the sun. <u>*In contrast*</u>, other systems use coal, oil, or nuclear energy.

Solar-powered systems have many advantages. <u>*However*</u>, a solar-powered system only works in locations where the sun shines many hours a day all year long.

Countries with ocean access can use desalination plants. <u>*However*</u>, other countries must find other solutions.

A. Read each sentence. Underline the word or phrase that shows a contrast.

1. Humans have one heart, <u>whereas</u> octopuses have three hearts.

2. Penguins live only in Antarctica; however, turtles live on every continent except Antarctica.

3. A human's heart is in his or her chest. In contrast, a shrimp's heart is in its head.

4. The humpback whale migrates 17,000 kilometers every year, but the arctic tern migrates 80,000 kilometers.

5. Sharks have existed for 400 million years. However, jellyfish have been around for 650 million years.

B. Complete each sentence with a contrasting idea. Compare your sentences with a partner.

1. Most people know that there is a shortage of water,

    but they continue to use too much   .

2. Studying oceanography is interesting,

    _____ .

3. Living near the ocean is expensive

    _____ .

4. A desalination system may be a good solution for an island country,

    _____ .

WRITING SKILL | Academic Language

LEARN

When you talk to your friends or write emails or blogs, you use everyday (informal) language. However, when you write for academic, business, or professional purposes, you need more formal language. Academic language is different from everyday language in several ways:

Everyday language ...	Academic language ...
• often uses the pronouns *I, you,* and *we* (*You can't drink salt water.*)	• may not use personal pronouns (*Salt water is not good to drink.*)
• uses contractions (*can't, won't, doesn't*)	• does not use contractions (*cannot, will not, does not*)
• includes questions and exclamations	• does not usually include questions and exclamations
• uses common vocabulary including slang and informal words (*a lot of, kids, stuff*)	• uses technical and academic vocabulary (*much, many, children, items*)
• is not always written in complete sentences	• is almost always written in complete sentences

APPLY

A. Reread the writing model on pages 114–115. Find examples of these features of academic language and share them with a partner.

1. avoiding personal pronouns: _____

2. avoiding contractions: _____

3. technical or academic vocabulary: _____

B. Find and circle sentences in the model with the same meaning as these sentences.

1. If we don't have water, we're going to have big problems.

2. First, you need to find a good place, so engineers check out a bunch of places to find a good spot.

3. They figure out how much water they can get from each system.

4. A system using the sun is better than other kinds of systems in a lot of ways.

5. It's too bad that you can't use these systems if your country isn't close to an ocean.

Collaborative Writing

A. Read the paragraph about another type of desalination. Underline all the features of everyday language.

Thirsty? How about a nice glass of salt water? Kids, I'm going to tell you how to make fresh water out of sea water. Just put salt water in a big bowl. Now, put an empty glass right in the middle of the bowl. Cover the bowl with plastic wrap. Don't forget to put a small hole in the middle of the plastic, over the glass. You then put the bowl in a sunny place. If you wait a few days, you'll have a glass of fresh water. Enjoy!

B. Draw a diagram of the process to help you and your readers understand it clearly.

C. Work with your partner to rewrite the paragraph using academic language.

1. Find the incomplete sentences and questions and rewrite them as complete sentences.

2. Remove the personal pronouns *I* and *you*.

3. Change some of the vocabulary to more technical language. For example, you could use the words *desalination, desalinated, option, direct sunlight*, and *drinking water*.

4. Write your paragraph. Start with a sentence that introduces the process. End your paragraph with an interesting sentence that summarizes the process.

D. Read your paragraph aloud to another group.

1. Are the steps in order and clear? If not, change the order and add signal words as necessary.

2. Does each sentence start with a signal word? If so, consider taking some out if the order is clear without them.

3. Check your verb tenses. Are they consistent? Change any that are not unless you can explain why it is necessary to use a different tense.

4. Have you used any of the target words from this unit?

Independent Writing

A. Choose a process you could write about for a science article. Choose from one of the processes below or use an idea of your own.

1. growing a plant from a seed

2. changing water from a liquid to a gas or to a solid

3. the natural process called the water cycle (rain, evaporation, etc.)

B. Use the chart below to write notes about each step in the process.

VOCABULARY TIP

As you outline the steps, write down technical words. Look them up in a dictionary or on the Internet. You may want to use some of these words in your article.

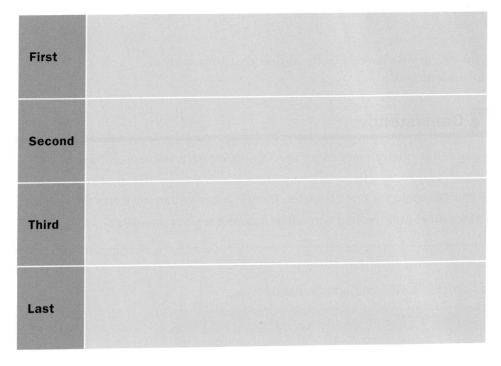

First	
Second	
Third	
Last	

C. What technical words does your reader need to know to understand your article? Write them, their definitions, and an example of each one in the chart below.

Technical Word	Definition	Example

D. Write notes about why the process is important. You can use this information in your introduction and conclusion.

E. Write your scientific magazine article. Use the chart in activity B to organize the steps in the process. Use your notes from activity D to create your introduction and conclusion. In your writing, use the target vocabulary words from page 113, time signal words from page 116, and technical words from activity C.

A. Read your article. Answer the questions below, and make revisions to your article as needed.

1. Check (✓) the information you included in your article.

   ☐ an introduction explaining why the process is important
   ☐ steps in the process
   ☐ a diagram to help readers understand the process
   ☐ explanations of any steps in the process that might be difficult for readers to understand

2. Look at the information you did not include. Would adding that information make your article easier to understand?

Grammar for Editing | Consistency

Consistency in writing means that related sentences use the same verb tense and have the same point of view.

| Not Consistent: | The water flows into the first container. There is a heater that will warm the water. |
| Consistent: | The water flows into the first container. A heater warms the water. |

B. Check the language in your article. Revise and edit as needed.

Language Checklist
☐ I used target vocabulary words in my article.
☐ I used academic language where appropriate.
☐ I used expressions of contrast correctly.
☐ My sentences are consistent in verb tense and point of view.

C. Check your article again. Repeat activities A and B.

Self-Assessment Review: Go back to page 113 and reassess your knowledge of the target vocabulary. How has your understanding of the words changed? What words do you feel most comfortable using now?

How Our Bodies Protect Us

In this unit, you will

> analyze a blog article and learn how it communicates information about physiology.

> use cause-and-effect writing.

> increase your understanding of the target academic words for this unit.

WRITING SKILLS

> Cause and Effect

> Paragraphing

> **GRAMMAR** Adverb Clauses of Reason and Result

Self-Assessment

Think about how well you know each target word, and check (✓) the appropriate column. I have…

TARGET WORDS	never seen this word before.	heard or seen the word but am not sure what it means.	heard or seen the word and understand what it means.	used the word confidently in *either* speaking or writing.
AWL				
🔑 confirm				
🔑 conflict				
🔑 deny				
🔑 equivalent				
flexible				
instruct				
🔑 medium				
modify				
🔑 reject				
submit				

🔑 Oxford 3000™ keywords

Building Knowledge

Read these questions. Discuss your answers in a small group.

1. How often do you yawn?

2. In what situations do you yawn?

3. Why do you think people yawn?

Writing Model

Blogs cover just about any subject you can imagine. Some blogs deal with health, behavior, or physiology. Read this blog article about yawning.

YAWNING: Bored, Sleepy, or Just Breathing?

I was sitting in class today when the **instructor** yawned. All of a sudden everyone in class was yawning. Why do we yawn after we see other people do it? And what is the use of yawning,
5 anyway? I decided to find out.

What are some reasons people yawn?

I started on the Internet. I found that people have **conflicting** beliefs about why we yawn. Some people think that we yawn because we're bored. Some think that we yawn because we're sleepy. Others think we yawn in order to stretch our muscles. However, most scientists believe that we yawn to give
10 our bodies extra oxygen.

It's like breathing. It's involuntary.[1] What would happen if you had to **instruct** your lungs to breathe or your eyes to blink? You wouldn't have time to think about anything else. Your body just does these things naturally.

So, is it all about breathing? If so, why do I yawn more when I'm tired or
15 bored? Studies **confirm** that when you're tired or bored, you tend to breathe more slowly. As a result, your body may not get all of the oxygen it needs to

[1] *involuntary:* done without wanting to or meaning to

work well. This sends a signal to your brain that makes you yawn. You may **deny** that you feel tired or bored. However, yawning makes you feel better.

A similar thing happens if you're in a room with a lot of other people. They're
20 all breathing the same air inside the room. After a while, the amount of oxygen in the air decreases. Your brain senses that you have not breathed in enough oxygen. It signals your lungs to take an extra big breath to get more oxygen into your body. Your **flexible** throat muscles stretch. Your eyes close. Your mouth opens wide, and you yawn. The yawn is **equivalent** to taking an
25 extra big breath.

Some scientists **reject** the idea that yawning is just about getting extra oxygen. They **submit** different ideas about why we yawn. One idea is that yawning **modifies** the temperature of the brain in order to keep it cool. Scientists have done experiments to prove this. In one experiment, scientists
30 put small bags of ice on the heads of half of the people in a **medium**-sized room. Soon the people without ice started yawning. But the people with the ice bags did not yawn as much as the others.

OK, so let's go back to my class full of yawning students. Scientists—and just about everyone else—agree that yawning is contagious.[2] This explains
35 why we all yawned when we saw our **instructor** yawn. Scientists believe we are more likely to yawn if we know the person who is yawning. However, the power of suggestion[3] is very strong. I sometimes yawn when I see an actor yawning on television or an Internet video. The suggestion is so strong that just thinking or reading about yawning makes some people yawn. If you have
40 yawned since you started reading this blog, then you understand what I'm telling you.

FREQUENCY OF CONTAGIOUS YAWNING ASSOCIATED WITH OTHERS

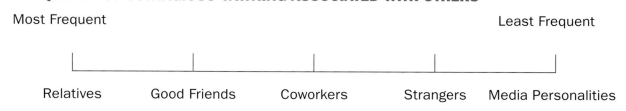

Most Frequent				Least Frequent
Relatives	Good Friends	Coworkers	Strangers	Media Personalities

---
[2] *contagious:* something contagious passes from one person to another
[3] *power of suggestion:* putting an idea into someone's mind

WRITING SKILL   Cause and Effect

LEARN

Articles about health often use cause-and-effect writing to describe how the human body works. Some articles focus on causes. They explain the reason things happen. Other articles focus on effects. They look at results. Some articles discuss both.

Cause	Effect
When I am tired,	I yawn.
Because I was bored,	I yawned.
I needed more air,	so I yawned.

Signal words help readers identify causes and effects of processes. The list below includes some common signal words used in cause-and-effect writing.

Words that signal causes	Words and phrases that signal effects
because	to, in order to
when	so, so that
	as a result

For cause-and-effect articles, use one of these methods of organization:

1. Cause → Effect → Cause → Effect (e.g., *When you are tired, you breathe slowly. Therefore, you have less oxygen,* etc.)

2. Effect → Causes (e.g., the causes of yawning)

3. Cause → Effects (e.g., the effects of a lack of oxygen)

If your article has more than one paragraph, you can use a different organization in each paragraph, as the writing model does.

APPLY

A. Circle any words in the writing model that signal cause and effect.

B. Reread the second paragraph. Complete the chart with causes of yawning.

1. Being bored	
2.	
3.	Yawning
4.	

C. Reread the fourth paragraph. Complete the chart with the causes and effects.

You're tired or bored.		Body doesn't get enough oxygen	

D. Reread the sixth paragraph. Check (✓) the correct boxes to show what happened in the experiment.

Group	Cause	Effect
People with ice on their heads	☐ Brains felt cool ☐ Brains felt hot	☐ Yawned ☐ Didn't yawn
People without ice on their heads	☐ Brains felt cool ☐ Brains felt hot	☐ Yawned ☐ Didn't yawn

Analyze

A. Complete the outline of the blog post. Use the labels from the box.

conflicting beliefs about yawning   ~~personal story~~   why and how we yawn
yawning is contagious   other scientists' opinion

Paragraph	Topic
1	*personal story*
2	
3–5	
6	
7	

B. Answer these questions with a partner.

1. How does the last paragraph help explain the story in the first paragraph?

_____

2. What information is in the graphic at the end of the blog post?

_____

3. Who is most likely to read this article?

_____

4. How is this blog different from an article about yawning in a scientific journal?

_____

The adjective *medium* describes "the size of something between small and big."

> *There was a **medium**-sized crowd in the theater.*

The noun *medium* refers to "a way of communicating." The plural form is usually *media*.

> *Radio is a broadcast **medium**. Magazines and newspapers are print **media**.*

The term *the media* refers to "television, radio, and newspapers used as a way to communicate."

> ***The media** report that the governor has signed the new budget.*

CORPUS

A. Complete the sentences by writing the word *medium* and a word from the box.

green	heat	height	size	weight

1. This color isn't dark green or light green. It's _medium green_ _____.

2. My brother isn't too tall or too short. He's _____.

3. That box is big, but it's not too heavy. It's only _____.

4. I need to buy a jacket. I wear a _____.

5. Cook the meat for 45 minutes over _____.

B. Complete the paragraph about a first-aid course for teachers. Use a form of *instruct* in each blank space. Compare your paragraph answers with a partner.

Word Form Chart		
Noun	**Verb**	**Adjective**
instructor instruction	instruct	instructive

The (1) _____ talked about playground injuries. She

(2) _____ us to always check an injured child for broken bones.

The (3) _____ gave each of us a brochure with (4) _____

on how to identify a concussion. The class included (5) _____ on

treating eye injuries. I learned a lot. The class was very (6) _____.

When you *reject* something, you "say that you do not want it." The phrase *to turn something down* is an informal way to express this idea.

> My son **rejected** my offer to help him. (He **turned down** my offer.)

> His **rejection** hurt my feelings.

When you *reject* an idea, you do not believe it.

> I **reject** the idea that yawning is contagious.

To *submit* something is "to give something important to an agency, person, etc." It often refers to something required or official.

> We have to **submit** our tax form by April 15.

> The **submission** deadline is April 15.

CORPUS

C. Complete this paragraph with forms of *reject* and *submit*.

When I graduated from high school, I (1) _____ the idea that I

needed a university degree. I was certain that I could get a good job without

a degree. I (2) _____ many job applications, but the companies

(3) _____ each one. After each (4) _____, I felt more

and more depressed. Finally, I gave up and (5) _____ an

application to a university. Imagine my disappointment when I received a

(6) _____ letter in the mail. But I (7) _____ another

application and was accepted into a good university. I now have a university

degree and a good job.

D. The list below shows measurements in the U.S. system and the metric system.
Match the measurement in the U.S. system to its *equivalent* in the metric system.
Compare answers with a partner. Use the word *equivalent*.

One foot is equivalent to .305 meters.

U.S. System	Metric System
_b_ 1. 1 foot	a. 0.946 liters
___ 2. 1 yard	b. 0.305 meters
___ 3. 1 quart	c. 01.61 kilometers
___ 4. 1 mile	d. 0.914 meters

To *conflict* (con-**FLICT**) means "to disagree or be different." It is often followed by the preposition *with*. The verb *conflict* can also refer to two events happening at the same time.

> Our answers **conflict**.

> My science class **conflicts** with my club meeting.

A *conflict* (**CON**-flict) is "a fight or an argument." The conflict can be very small or it can be large. A conflict can also be a difference between two ideas.

> The doctors had a **conflict** over what causes yawning.

E. **Complete the paragraph. Use a form of *conflict* in each blank space.**

There is a (1) _____ going on between the magazine *A Healthy You* and the magazine *To Your Health*. The two magazines often print health advice that (2) _____. For example, one magazine says that everyone should drink eight glasses of water every day. The other prints (3) _____ advice, saying that you need water only when you're thirsty. There is also a (4) _____ over how much sleep people need. One magazine says that your body knows when it's time to wake up. The other has (5) _____ information. It says everyone should sleep eight hours every night.

Vocabulary Activities STEP II: Sentence Level

The words *deny* and *confirm* have opposite meanings.

When you *deny* something, you say that it is not true. The noun form is *denial*.

> Mike **denied** that he was bored.

> However, he yawned when he made the **denial**.

When you *confirm* something, you say that it is true. The noun form is *confirmation*.

> Mariah **confirmed** that she was bored.

> Her yawn was **confirmation**.

To *deny somebody* means "to not allow the person to have or do something."

> The nurse **denied** the patient food before the exam.

To *confirm something* is used to say that something will happen.

> Pham called the doctor's office to **confirm** his appointment.

F. Rewrite the numbered sentences using the words in parentheses.

Pham arrived at the office on time. (1) He showed his medical card to prove his identity. (2) A nurse said, "I want to make sure that you are here for an operation." (3) Pham said that he was not there for an operation. He needed an X-ray of his foot. The doctor X-rayed Pham's foot. (4) The doctor said that the X-ray showed that Pham's toe was broken. (5) The doctor refused Pham's request for a wheelchair and said he would be fine with crutches.

1. (confirm) _He showed his medical card to confirm his identity._

2. (confirm) _____

3. (denied) _____

4. (confirmed) _____

5. (denied) _____

If something is *flexible*, you can change it easily. The opposite is *inflexible*.

> My new boss allows me to work **flexible** hours. My old boss was very **inflexible**.

When an object is *flexible*, it can bend easily without breaking.

> Plastic is often used in plumbing because it is **flexible** enough to fit in small spaces.

When you *modify* something, you change it. *Modification* is the noun form.

> I have to **modify** our plans for tomorrow. I can't come at nine. Is ten o'clock OK?

CORPUS

G. Rewrite each numbered sentence using the word in parentheses.

I recently joined a gym. (1) I want my arms and legs to move easily when I play tennis. (2) I'll change my diet so I can lose weight, too. I decided to go to the gym every day. (3) Fortunately, my work schedule is easy to change.

1. (flexible) _I want my arms and legs to be flexible when I play tennis._

2. (modify) _____

3. (flexible) _____

We use adverb clauses to explain why people do things. Adverb clauses can express reasons and results.

Adverb Clauses of Reason

Many adverb clauses of reason use the words *because* or *when* to tell why something happens.

We yawn <u>because</u> we are bored.   <u>When</u> we are bored, we yawn.

Adverb Clauses of Result

An adverb clause with the words *so* (adjective/adverb) *that* shows a result.

I was <u>*so tired that*</u> I couldn't stop yawning.   Alex was <u>*so cold that*</u> he began to shake.

A. Reread the writing model. Underline one example of an adverb clause of reason with *because* and one adverb clause of result with *so . . . that*.

B. Work with a partner. Use *because, so that,* or *so . . . that* to combine the two sentences into one sentence.

1. The student was bored. She just looked out the window.

   The student was so bored that she just looked out the window.

2. The gymnast was flexible. She could easily touch her hands to the floor.

   _____

3. The students were yawning. The teacher decided to open all of the windows.

   _____

4. I had to apply to several more universities. My first choice school rejected me.

   _____

C. Complete the sentences with your own words using *so . . . that*. Then compare your sentences with a partner.

1. _____*I was so cold that*_____ my eyes started to water.

2. _____ she started to cry.

3. _____ I was sweating heavily.

4. _____ I blinked several times when I walked outside.

WRITING SKILL | Paragraphing

LEARN

A paragraph is a series of sentences about one idea. As you write, you need to think about how to divide your ideas into paragraphs. Good paragraphing helps readers understand the organization of your ideas. Each paragraph should communicate one idea.

Start a new paragraph when

- you have finished your introduction or you are starting your conclusion.

- you introduce a new idea.

- you want to draw attention to an idea or example.

- you present a contrasting point or view.

APPLY

Work with a partner. Discuss the following questions about the writing model on page 128–129.

1. Read the first and second paragraphs. Why are these separate paragraphs? Could they be combined into one paragraph? Why, or why not?

2. The third, fourth, and fifth paragraphs all relate to how and why we yawn. What is the purpose of each paragraph?

3. Which paragraph presents a contrasting point of view?

Collaborative Writing

A. Work with a partner. Read the incomplete paragraph. It is the first of two paragraphs about blinking. What is the main idea?

You probably never think about it, but you blink your eyes about 14 to 17 times per minute. Like breathing or your heart beating, blinking is an important involuntary action. Why is blinking so important? There are several reasons for natural blinking. First, when you blink, your eyelids close over your eyes. When they close, they spread moisture over your eyes. Blinking keeps your eyes from becoming too dry.

_____

_____

_____

B. The notes below are additional ideas to add to the article. Decide how to finish the first paragraph on page 137 and what information to include in the second paragraph. Write the number 1 next to ideas that should be in the first paragraph. Write the number 2 next to ideas that should go in the second paragraph.

_____ a. reasons for excessive (too much) blinking

_____ b. eyes are too dry; smoke or dust in the air

_____ c. blinking protects the eyes from dust

_____ d. if your eyes are watering (due to allergies), it will cause you to blink more

_____ e. young children with vision problems

_____ f. if person is under pressure—nervous

_____ g. psychological conditions may cause excessive blinking (Examples: stress or tiredness)

_____ h. protects the eyes from strong sunlight or change in temperature

C. Work with a partner to finish the first paragraph, writing on the lines in activity A on page 137. Then write the second paragraph. Include the ideas from activity B.

D. Compare your paragraphs with the paragraphs of another pair of students. How are your paragraphs similar? How are they different? Can you improve your paragraphs?

Independent Writing

A. Plan a paragraph about the causes of tears. (If you prefer, you can write about sneezing or coughing.)

Use this chart to brainstorm some of the things that cause tears to form in a person's eyes.

Causes of involuntary tears:	• Extreme cold
Other causes of tears:	• Fear

B. For each cause, write notes about details or examples you can add. Write down how you might explain those causes.

C. Look up any words from the Vocabulary Tip box that you do not know. Then decide which ones relate to what you are writing about.

D. Begin your article with a brief description of the effect (tears). What happens when a person's eyes water?

E. Complete with information you might want to include.

_____ can make you your eyes water.

People often cry when they _____.

_____ is a common cause of tears.

People often have tears when they _____.

Sometimes people have tears because they _____.

F. Write your blog article. Use your list of causes to help organize your information into at least two paragraphs. In your writing, try to use the target vocabulary words from page 127 and include cause-and-effect signal words.

A. Read your blog article. Answer the questions below, and make revisions to your blog article as needed.

1. Check (✓) the information that you included in your blog article.

   ☐ an introduction describing the effect
   ☐ an explanation of several causes
   ☐ words to identify the causes
   ☐ sentences that clearly show the cause-and-effect relationship

2. Look at the information you did not include. Would adding that information clarify the cause-and-effect relationship?

Grammar for Editing Punctuating Adverb Clauses

Adverb clauses can be found at the beginning of a sentence, in the middle of a sentence, or at the end of a sentence.

At the beginning of a sentence, adverb clauses are followed by a comma.

> **Because we are bored, we yawn.**

In the middle of a sentence, adverb clauses are set off by commas.

> **My friends, because they were tired, yawned.**

At the end of a sentence, adverb clauses usually don't require a comma.

> **We yawn because we are bored.**

B. Check the language in your blog article. Revise and edit as needed.

Language Checklist
☐ I used target vocabulary words where they were appropriate.
☐ I used appropriate vocabulary to describe tears.
☐ I used words of cause and effect correctly.
☐ I punctuated adverb clauses correctly.

C. Check your blog article again. Repeat activities A and B.

Self-Assessment Review: Go back to page 127 and reassess your knowledge of the target vocabulary. How has your understanding of the words changed? What words do you feel most comfortable using now?

The Academic Word List

Words targeted in Level 1 are bold

Word	Sublist	Location
abandon	8	L2, U6
abstract	6	L3, U1
academy	5	L2, U8
access	4	L0, U6
accommodate	9	L3, U6
accompany	8	L4, U6
accumulate	8	L3, U10
accurate	6	L0, U4
achieve	2	L0, U1
acknowledge	6	L0, U7
acquire	2	L3, U4
adapt	7	L0, U3
adequate	4	L3, U3
adjacent	10	L4, U3
adjust	5	L4, U6
administrate	2	L4, U10
adult	7	L0, U8
advocate	7	L4, U4
affect	**2**	**L1, U2**
aggregate	6	L4, U5
aid	7	L3, U4
albeit	10	L4, U9
allocate	6	L3, U1
alter	5	L2, U6
alternative	**3**	**L1, U7**
ambiguous	8	L4, U7
amend	5	L4, U1
analogy	9	L4, U2
analyze	**1**	**L1, U9**
annual	**4**	**L1, U6**
anticipate	9	L2, U5
apparent	4	L2, U5
append	8	L4, U9
appreciate	8	L0, U8
approach	**1**	**L1, U2**
appropriate	2	L3, U4
approximate	4	L2, U1
arbitrary	8	L4, U7
area	1	L0, U6
aspect	2	L2, U3
assemble	10	L3, U6
assess	1	L2, U4
assign	6	L3, U9
assist	2	L0, U4
assume	1	L3, U4
assure	9	L3, U9
attach	6	L0, U7

Word	Sublist	Location
attain	9	L3, U5
attitude	4	L2, U4
attribute	4	L3, U3
author	6	L0, U9
authority	1	L2, U9
automate	8	L2, U5
available	1	L0, U8
aware	**5**	**L1, U3**
behalf	9	L4, U1
benefit	1	L2, U4
bias	8	L4, U2
bond	6	L4, U9
brief	6	L2, U4
bulk	9	L3, U1
capable	6	L3, U7
capacity	5	L4, U2
category	2	L2, U3
cease	9	L2, U8
challenge	**5**	**L1, U2**
channel	7	L4, U3
chapter	2	L0, U9
chart	8	L0, U8
chemical	7	L2, U10
circumstance	3	L4, U3
cite	6	L4, U7
civil	4	L3, U10
clarify	8	L3, U8
classic	7	L3, U9
clause	5	L3, U3
code	4	L0, U7
coherent	9	L4, U6
coincide	9	L4, U6
collapse	10	L3, U6
colleague	10	L3, U1
commence	9	L2, U9
comment	**3**	**L1, U5**
commission	2	L4, U2
commit	4	L2, U2
commodity	8	L4, U10
communicate	**4**	**L1, U3**
community	**2**	**L1, U4**
compatible	9	L2, U3
compensate	3	L4, U8
compile	10	L3, U2
complement	8	L4, U9

Oxford 3000™

Word	Sublist	Location
🔑 complex	2	L3, U10
🔑 component	3	L3, U3
compound	5	L3, U10
comprehensive	7	L3, U3
comprise	7	L3, U1
compute	**2**	**L1, U7**
conceive	10	L4, U4
🔑 **concentrate**	**4**	**L1, U2**
🔑 concept	1	L3, U9
🔑 conclude	2	L0, U2
concurrent	9	L4, U3
🔑 **conduct**	**2**	**L1, U5**
confer	4	L4, U9
confine	9	L4, U4
🔑 **confirm**	**7**	**L1, U10**
🔑 **conflict**	**5**	**L1, U10**
conform	8	L3, U8
consent	3	L3, U7
consequent	2	L4, U7
🔑 considerable	3	L3, U9
🔑 **consist**	**1**	**L1, U1**
🔑 **constant**	**3**	**L1, U7**
constitute	1	L4, U1
constrain	3	L4, U5
🔑 construct	2	L2, U1
🔑 consult	5	L2, U2
consume	2	L2, U6
🔑 **contact**	**5**	**L1, U3**
🔑 contemporary	8	L4, U3
🔑 context	1	L2, U4
🔑 contract	1	L3, U4
contradict	8	L2, U4
contrary	7	L3, U8
🔑 contrast	4	L3, U5
🔑 **contribute**	**3**	**L1, U4**
controversy	9	L2, U1
convene	3	L4, U8
converse	9	L2, U10
🔑 convert	7	L4, U9
🔑 **convince**	**10**	**L1, U9**
cooperate	6	L3, U2
coordinate	3	L2, U5
🔑 core	3	L4, U1
corporate	**3**	**L1, U7**
correspond	3	L3, U2
🔑 couple	7	L0, U7
🔑 create	1	L2, U7
🔑 credit	2	L2, U9
🔑 criteria	3	L3, U3
🔑 crucial	8	L4, U4
🔑 culture	2	L0, U9

Word	Sublist	Location
currency	8	L2, U7
🔑 cycle	4	L3, U1
🔑 data	1	L0, U3
🔑 debate	4	L3, U5
🔑 **decade**	**7**	**L1, U9**
🔑 **decline**	**5**	**L1, U6**
deduce	3	L3, U3
🔑 define	1	L0, U6
🔑 definite	7	L4, U6
🔑 **demonstrate**	**3**	**L1, U5**
denote	8	L4, U10
🔑 **deny**	**7**	**L1, U10**
🔑 depress	10	L0, U10
🔑 derive	1	L4, U2
🔑 design	2	L0, U3
🔑 despite	4	L3, U10
detect	8	L2, U1
deviate	8	L4, U7
🔑 device	9	L0, U7
🔑 devote	9	L2, U4
differentiate	7	L3, U8
dimension	4	L4, U9
diminish	9	L2, U6
discrete	5	L4, U10
discriminate	6	L4, U1
displace	8	L3, U5
🔑 display	6	L0, U9
dispose	7	L4, U8
distinct	2	L4, U10
distort	9	L4, U7
🔑 **distribute**	**1**	**L1, U6**
diverse	6	L4, U3
🔑 document	3	L0, U10
domain	6	L4, U7
🔑 domestic	4	L2, U6
🔑 dominate	3	L4, U8
🔑 draft	5	L0, U10
🔑 drama	8	L2, U7
duration	9	L2, U5
dynamic	7	L3, U1
🔑 economy	1	L2, U3
edit	**6**	**L1, U1**
🔑 element	2	L3, U9
🔑 **eliminate**	**7**	**L1, U7**
🔑 emerge	4	L4, U10
🔑 **emphasis**	**3**	**L1, U7**
empirical	7	L4, U5
🔑 enable	5	L2, U7
🔑 **encounter**	**10**	**L1, U5**

Word	Sublist	Location
energy	5	L0, U1
enforce	5	L4, U7
enhance	6	L3, U5
enormous	10	L0, U2
ensure	3	L4, U6
entity	5	L4, U9
environment	**1**	**L1, U6**
equate	2	L3, U2
equip	7	L2, U3
equivalent	**5**	**L1, U10**
erode	9	L4, U8
error	4	L0, U4
establish	1	L2, U2
estate	6	L3, U1
estimate	1	L2, U8
ethic	9	L3, U8
ethnic	4	L3, U10
evaluate	**2**	**L1, U8**
eventual	8	L3, U5
evident	1	L2, U1
evolve	5	L2, U8
exceed	**6**	**L1, U8**
exclude	3	L2, U2
exhibit	8	L2, U10
expand	5	L0, U2
expert	6	L2, U2
explicit	6	L4, U7
exploit	8	L4, U7
export	1	L3, U9
expose	5	L4, U8
external	5	L2, U3
extract	7	L3, U5
facilitate	5	L3, U6
factor	1	L3, U2
feature	2	L0, U5
federal	6	L4, U1
fee	6	L0, U5
file	7	L0, U10
final	2	L0, U3
finance	1	L3, U4
finite	7	L4, U9
flexible	**6**	**L1, U10**
fluctuate	8	L4, U6
focus	2	L0, U1
format	9	L2, U1
formula	1	L3, U8
forthcoming	10	L4, U9
found	9	L0, U10
foundation	**7**	**L1, U9**
framework	3	L4, U3

Word	Sublist	Location
function	1	L3, U3
fund	3	L2, U9
fundamental	**5**	**L1, U8**
furthermore	6	L3, U1
gender	6	L3, U2
generate	**5**	**L1, U4**
generation	5	L2, U8
globe	7	L2, U1
goal	4	L0, U1
grade	7	L0, U9
grant	4	L3, U2
guarantee	**7**	**L1, U4**
guideline	**8**	**L1, U8**
hence	4	L3, U1
hierarchy	7	L4, U10
highlight	8	L0, U7
hypothesis	4	L3, U7
identical	7	L3, U7
identify	**1**	**L1, U5**
ideology	7	L4, U3
ignorance	6	L2, U10
illustrate	3	L0, U6
image	**5**	**L1, U7**
immigrate	3	L4, U8
impact	2	L2, U6
implement	4	L4, U7
implicate	4	L3, U7
implicit	8	L4, U1
imply	3	L3, U5
impose	4	L3, U8
incentive	6	L4, U5
incidence	6	L3, U2
incline	10	L4, U6
income	1	L3, U2
incorporate	6	L4, U3
index	6	L4, U8
indicate	1	L2, U3
individual	1	L0, U4
induce	8	L4, U4
inevitable	8	L4, U1
infer	7	L4, U2
infrastructure	8	L4, U10
inherent	9	L4, U5
inhibit	6	L4, U5
initial	3	L0, U4
initiate	6	L3, U2
injure	2	L4, U6
innovate	7	L3, U3

Word	Sublist	Location
input	6	L2, U2
insert	7	L2, U7
insight	9	L3, U7
inspect	8	L4, U7
instance	3	L3, U4
institute	**2**	**L1, U8**
instruct	**6**	**L1, U10**
integral	9	L4, U5
integrate	4	L4, U7
integrity	10	L2, U8
intelligence	6	L0, U8
intense	8	L3, U7
interact	3	L2, U1
intermediate	9	L2, U7
internal	**4**	**L1, U2**
interpret	1	L4, U2
interval	6	L3, U7
intervene	7	L3, U4
intrinsic	10	L4, U5
invest	2	L3, U9
investigate	4	L2, U9
invoke	10	L4, U9
involve	1	L3, U10
isolate	7	L3, U4
issue	1	L0, U6
item	2	L0, U5
job	4	L0, U3
journal	**2**	**L1, U9**
justify	3	L3, U2
label	4	L0, U5
labor	1	L2, U4
layer	3	L4, U10
lecture	6	L0, U8
legal	**1**	**L1, U3**
legislate	1	L4, U1
levy	10	L4, U4
liberal	5	L4, U3
license	5	L3, U6
likewise	10	L3, U10
link	3	L0, U5
locate	**3**	**L1, U1**
logic	5	L3, U1
maintain	**2**	**L1, U4**
major	1	L0, U2
manipulate	8	L4, U2
manual	9	L3, U3
margin	5	L2, U4
mature	9	L2, U8

Word	Sublist	Location
maximize	**3**	**L1, U7**
mechanism	4	L3, U3
media	7	L0, U9
mediate	9	L3, U4
medical	**5**	**L1, U2**
medium	**9**	**L1, U10**
mental	5	L2, U10
method	**1**	**L1, U3**
migrate	6	L4, U10
military	9	L2, U9
minimal	**9**	**L1, U8**
minimize	8	L3, U9
minimum	**6**	**L1, U8**
ministry	6	L4, U1
minor	3	L0, U8
mode	7	L3, U2
modify	**5**	**L1, U10**
monitor	5	L3, U7
motive	6	L2, U4
mutual	9	L2, U10
negate	3	L4, U8
network	5	L2, U5
neutral	6	L2, U9
nevertheless	6	L3, U10
nonetheless	10	L4, U6
norm	9	L4, U5
normal	2	L0, U3
notion	5	L4, U2
notwithstanding	10	L4, U2
nuclear	8	L3, U10
objective	5	L0, U4
obtain	2	L3, U1
obvious	**4**	**L1, U5**
occupy	4	L4, U6
occur	1	L2, U1
odd	**10**	**L1, U1**
offset	8	L3, U2
ongoing	10	L2, U5
option	**4**	**L1, U9**
orient	5	L4, U7
outcome	3	L2, U4
output	4	L2, U3
overall	4	L2, U3
overlap	9	L2, U9
overseas	6	L3, U10
panel	10	L4, U1
paradigm	7	L4, U9
paragraph	**8**	**L1, U1**

Word	Sublist	Location
parallel	4	L4, U10
parameter	4	L3, U8
participate	**2**	**L1, U1**
partner	3	L0, U5
passive	9	L3, U8
perceive	2	L4, U6
percent	**1**	**L1, U7**
period	1	L3, U4
persist	10	L3, U7
perspective	5	L2, U3
phase	4	L2, U1
phenomenon	7	L4, U5
philosophy	3	L3, U9
physical	3	L0, U1
plus	8	L0, U6
policy	1	L2, U8
portion	9	L2, U6
pose	10	L4, U2
positive	2	L0, U1
potential	2	L2, U5
practitioner	8	L4, U4
precede	6	L3, U8
precise	5	L3, U9
predict	4	L0, U3
predominant	8	L4, U10
preliminary	9	L2, U5
presume	6	L4, U6
previous	2	L0, U5
primary	**2**	**L1, U4**
prime	5	L4, U6
principal	4	L2, U7
principle	1	L3, U8
prior	4	L2, U9
priority	7	L2, U5
proceed	1	L2, U7
process	**1**	**L1, U5**
professional	**4**	**L1, U8**
prohibit	7	L3, U5
project	**4**	**L1, U1**
promote	4	L4, U4
proportion	3	L2, U6
prospect	8	L4, U2
protocol	9	L4, U8
psychology	5	L2, U6
publication	7	L3, U7
publish	3	L0, U10
purchase	2	L0, U5
pursue	5	L4, U1
qualitative	9	L4, U5
quote	**7**	**L1, U9**
radical	8	L4, U2
random	8	L2, U10
range	2	L2, U3
ratio	5	L3, U6
rational	6	L3, U8
react	**3**	**L1, U5**
recover	6	L2, U5
refine	9	L3, U1
regime	4	L3, U10
region	2	L3, U10
register	3	L3, U9
regulate	2	L3, U3
reinforce	8	L3, U6
reject	**5**	**L1, U10**
relax	9	L0, U4
release	**7**	**L1, U6**
relevant	2	L3, U2
reluctance	10	L2, U8
rely	3	L2, U6
remove	3	L0, U8
require	1	L0, U3
research	1	L0, U2
reside	2	L4, U4
resolve	4	L2, U4
resource	2	L0, U4
respond	**1**	**L1, U4**
restore	8	L2, U5
restrain	9	L3, U6
restrict	2	L2, U6
retain	4	L4, U8
reveal	6	L2, U10
revenue	5	L3, U9
reverse	7	L3, U4
revise	**8**	**L1, U8**
revolution	9	L4, U3
rigid	9	L2, U8
role	1	L0, U7
route	9	L3, U10
scenario	9	L2, U8
schedule	**7**	**L1, U2**
scheme	3	L4, U8
scope	6	L2, U10
section	1	L0, U2
sector	1	L4, U9
secure	**2**	**L1, U4**
seek	2	L2, U9
select	**2**	**L1, U6**
sequence	**3**	**L1, U6**
series	4	L0, U2
sex	3	L4, U5

Oxford 3000™

Word	Sublist	Location
🔑 shift	3	L2, U7
🔑 significant	1	L3, U7
🔑 **similar**	**1**	**L1, U6**
simulate	7	L3, U3
🔑 **site**	**2**	**L1, U1**
so-called	10	L2, U1
sole	7	L4, U4
🔑 somewhat	7	L3, U5
🔑 **source**	**1**	**L1, U6**
🔑 **specific**	**1**	**L1, U3**
specify	**3**	**L1, U9**
sphere	9	L4, U2
🔑 stable	5	L3, U6
statistic	4	L2, U10
🔑 status	4	L0, U9
straightforward	10	L3, U3
🔑 strategy	2	L2, U2
🔑 stress	4	L0, U1
🔑 structure	1	L2, U7
🔑 style	5	L2, U2
submit	**7**	**L1, U10**
subordinate	9	L4, U9
subsequent	4	L3, U5
subsidy	6	L4, U3
🔑 substitute	5	L2, U6
successor	7	L3, U8
🔑 sufficient	3	L4, U1
🔑 sum	4	L3, U5
🔑 **summary**	**4**	**L1, U3**
supplement	9	L2, U10
🔑 survey	2	L2, U9
🔑 survive	7	L2, U8
suspend	9	L4, U1
sustain	5	L3, U6
🔑 symbol	5	L0, U10
🔑 tape	6	L3, U5
🔑 target	5	L2, U2
🔑 task	3	L0, U6
🔑 team	9	L0, U1
🔑 technical	3	L3, U6
🔑 technique	3	L3, U6
🔑 technology	3	L2, U3
🔑 temporary	9	L0, U6
tense	7	L2, U1
terminate	7	L4, U8
🔑 text	2	L0, U10
🔑 **theme**	**7**	**L1, U9**
🔑 theory	1	L3, U7
thereby	7	L4, U6
thesis	7	L3, U7

Word	Sublist	Location
🔑 topic	7	L0, U7
🔑 trace	6	L4, U10
🔑 tradition	2	L0, U9
🔑 **transfer**	**2**	**L1, U6**
🔑 transform	6	L3, U1
transit	5	L2, U2
transmit	7	L4, U10
🔑 **transport**	**6**	**L1, U8**
🔑 **trend**	**5**	**L1, U3**
trigger	9	L4, U4
🔑 ultimate	7	L3, U9
undergo	10	L4, U4
underlie	6	L4, U5
undertake	4	L4, U3
🔑 uniform	7	L2, U10
unify	9	L2, U9
🔑 unique	7	L2, U7
utilize	6	L3, U6
🔑 valid	3	L3, U8
🔑 **vary**	**1**	**L1, U2**
🔑 vehicle	7	L2, U2
🔑 **version**	**5**	**L1, U9**
🔑 via	7	L4, U3
violate	9	L3, U6
virtual	8	L3, U5
🔑 visible	7	L0, U2
🔑 vision	9	L2, U2
visual	8	L2, U7
🔑 **volume**	**3**	**L1, U7**
voluntary	7	L3, U4
welfare	5	L4, U4
🔑 whereas	5	L4, U5
whereby	10	L4, U8
widespread	7	L3, U4

🔑 Oxford 3000™